D0064993

THE

INTERNATIONAL SERIES

IN THE BEHAVIORAL SCIENCES

EDITED BY

John E. Horrocks

THE OHIO STATE UNIVERSITY

*Houghton Mifflin books in Psychology
are under the general editorship of*

LEONARD CARMICHAEL

Gardner Murphy

Herbert E. Spohn
The Menninger Foundation

Encounter

with Reality

New Forms for an Old Quest

Houghton Mifflin Company · Boston

New York · Atlanta · Geneva, Ill. · Dallas · Palo Alto

To

JESSICA

and

MADELEINE

PERMISSIONS

The authors extend grateful thanks to the following publishers for permission to quote from the indicated materials:

Alfred A. Knopf, Inc., A. Camus, The Fall, (*Transl. J. O'Brien*), 1956. *Random House, Inc., F. Dostoyevsky,* The Brothers Karamazov, (*Transl. C. Garnett*), 1946. *University Books, W. F. Prince,* Noted Witnesses for Psychic Occurrences, 1963.

Editor's Foreword

Man is his own mystery. His endeavors to look inward and explain himself have been an enduring preoccupation across the ages. In his early days, man's experience could give him little scope for reading the riddle he posed. His chief weapons were his powers of observation of the molar phenomena of nature and the power of his own mind to speculate on what he had observed. His thinking was largely magical, and he attributed human or godlike causation to the events of nature. Natural phenomena such as thunderstorms were viewed as manifestations of the gods. But man could not conceive of his kinship with nature: he looked upon himself as something apart, in turn the victim and the beneficiary of the gods. He recognized that he was mortal, but saw himself as a reflection of the image of the gods and spent much of his time trying to bridge the gap between his own mortality and their immortality.

However, a counterinfluence was always at work. Man is a thinking, analyzing, hypothesizing animal. Over the centuries man has posed fundamental questions as to the terms of his existence and has come to cultivate doubt as a tool of inquiry. He designed instruments and techniques to examine himself and his surroundings in scientific rather than metaphysical terms. The invention of the microscope and the beginnings of science enabled him to learn more about himself as a mechanism and showed him that, rather than standing aside from nature, he was part of it. But as his understanding of the physical world and of his own physiology increased, man seemed to progress no further in understanding himself as a psychological organism. With the advent of psychology and its associated sciences, man has been studied more intensively in his every aspect. Many clues now exist that may one day lead to the ultimate answer, and there have been many attempts — like Sir Charles Sherrington's *Man on his Nature* and C. Judson Herrick's *The Evolution of Human Nature* — to piece these clues together. Yet the mystery remains.

Psychology has grappled with the great problems of the relation of mind and body, the meaning of awareness, and the nature of reality. It is with the last of these, man's encounter with reality, that the authors of this book have concerned themselves. Reality is a concept that has presented difficulties to everyone who has tried to come to grips with it. Even as he spatially occupies an outer world, every man has his inner world, which he has to construe not only as it exists at the moment but as it has existed and will exist across space and time. What is real, and what is not? What are the criteria for reality? Indeed, can anything exist that is not real, and, conversely, if it is real, can it fail to exist? But this question has within it the element of circularity, for it raises in turn the question, what are the criteria of existence?

As Murphy and Spohn see it, the dimensions of reality are a matter of personal relevance. Some things seem more and some less "real," and the psychic system of man encompasses them all. Some things are too real, some not real enough. Reality can be enhanced, and it can be overshadowed. One construes reality and perpetually edits it. To a large degree, man can control reality — even as he can create, he can destroy; and sometimes he is defenseless, and reality can be imposed upon him. But of all man's activities, the struggle to come to terms with reality is at the apex of his experience. It is the search for the real that engages man's energies because it poses the central question of his existence. Yet nothing is so highly personal as reality. Of any man we must ask, what kinds of reality is he capable of defining and pursuing, and, of course, what does he actually pursue?

Science has brought us to the point where we can say that there is something in the total system which "corresponds" to a reality as man construes it.

In *Encounter With Reality* the authors have approached the heart of the riddle of man's nature and have joined the company of those who have stood on the frontiers of understanding man.

JOHN E. HORROCKS

Columbus, Ohio

Preface

The philosophers of East and West have always hoped to escape from delusion and self-deception, seeking by one route or another an answer to the problem: "Can man know reality?" The purpose of this book is to note the changes in emphasis made necessary by the modern era in approaching this ancient problem. Such changes in emphasis are forced upon us by the evolutionary viewpoint, by the use of empirical methods in the investigation of perception and cognition, and by what has been learned of social and personal biases molding the form of the experienced world. But we seek to do more here than to state, in terms of experimental, clinical, and developmental psychology, issues which have classically belonged to metaphysics and epistemology. We seek to show that the question itself, "Can man know reality?" is subject to a new perspective, a new relativism. Thus we suggest the possibility of a new scientific approach, not only to the relation of man to the world, but also to the very processes by which he ventures to find a "real" reality.

The answer is not simple, nor shall we claim that man can directly and completely know reality. Indeed, we anticipate that an investigation of the processes of knowing will set certain limits as to what we can claim really to know. Thus this book is organized into two parts. Part One is in large measure concerned with the barriers in the way of objectivity imposed by the biological, personal, and cultural roots of human modes of knowing. It seeks to show the relativities and limitations in the advance toward reality. But in Part Two we turn to the positive directions established in this search and attempt an interpretation of what can actually be known about the environment and about man.

We are profoundly grateful for the close reading and helpful suggestions by Gordon W. Allport, Gordon L. Mangan, Henry A. Murray, and Charles M. Solley.

G.M.
H.E.S.

The Menninger Foundation
Topeka, Kansas

Contents

PART

ONE

1

Towards Reality

As a dominant and insistent theme, the term "reality" will recur throughout this book. It is a term rich in meanings and connotations. Therefore, it behooves us, at the beginning, to help the reader gain clarity about the meaning that "reality" has for us. And in the process of providing this clarification, we shall be foreshadowing the major areas of focus and the points of view our book offers.

First of all we shall deal with reality in evolutionary terms, seeking to find out how living things make contact with their environment and how they may fail to do so. From this vantage point, reality is the external environment to which the organism must adapt in order to survive. Organisms are endowed, in part by virtue of their evolutionary history, with more or less elaborate sensory equipment and a more or less complex nervous system through which reality is mediated. Upon the use of this equipment in making contact with the environment, in maintaining contact with it, in constructing it or adapting to it, depends the organism's integrity as organism and the survival of the species. Reality contact, thus, is conceived as commerce with external objects, which while incompletely known by the organism, and filtered through perceptual and cognitive processes, are nonetheless those upon which survival depends. From this point of view, the decisive criterion of the adequacy, completeness, or appropriateness of reality construction is a pragmatic one; namely, the survival of the individual organism, of species, and ultimately, of culture.

In viewing evolutionary history, however, we see *more* than simply the rise and fall of species meeting the challenge of adaptation to the environment more or less successfully, species selected for survival when their morphology, their sensory and integrative organs, cope effectively with the peculiarities of the particular real environment into which they have evolved. We see a pattern of evolutionary development in which more and more terrestrial environments are populated with organisms equipped to meet the peculiar adaptive requirements the conditions of survival in such environments pose. We see also that one major evolutionary trend in the development of organisms has been towards increasing complexity both of their sensory equipment and of the organs which integrate sensory messages, beginning with brain stem and spinal cord. For us this is a particularly significant trend: that, given the instability and modifiability of the "germ cell," those directions of development have been selected which progressively enrich and complicate the process of adaptation to the environment. There is, indeed, in man an urge for more than sensory-sensual contact with the world. This urge is best characterized as the need to make complex contact with the world, the need of the perceptual-cognitive system to apprehend systematic relationships.

Thus we shall conceive man's orientation to his environment, man's encounter with reality, not merely as a reality-coping one, centered essentially around the challenge of survival, but indeed also as a reality-seeking orientation, a demand to apprehend, to understand, to clarify, to conceptualize the complexities of his existence within the context of an external environment and through the filter of his as yet not fully known and fully understood inner environment.

We shall be concerned primarily with *man* as the most complex outcome of a long process of evolutionary history, and with man's encounter with reality. We shall approach the account of man's encounter with reality from at least two major underlying perspectives.

One of these perspectives is phenomenological, and through it we shall view all that has existence in the life space, the sphere of awareness of individuals. Under certain conditions impressions are made on the individual such as to lead him to assume the reality of objects or events although later he may find that these events or objects have no existence. Individuals may create trouble for themselves by saying that the impressions, hallucinations, illusions, etc., are "unreal." In point of fact, however, the hallucinations may be very real — may be real enough to cause suicide. The object believed to be real may turn out to be a figment of the imagination. But it is the external object that is unreal, not the impression or belief, or the mode of commerce with the environment. We shall extend the term "real" to all that has existence in this sense. Consequently we shall include, as our study develops, both objects and events in the so-called "outer world" and objects and events in the personal or "subjective world."

Though objects and events must be either real or unreal in this sense, their apprehension or a response to them may yield a series of steps which are truly *degrees of acceptance* of the thing as real. The death of a friend this week is real. The death of a famine-stricken child in India is less real. There are not then, in fact, *levels of reality*. Rather, there are gradations in attitudes of acceptance or rejection, that is, levels of personal relevance.

While our use of the term "reality" will have, in its broadest sense, reference to all the phenomena of experience, we also accept the reality of an outer world "in itself" — a world of objects *beyond* phenomena, self-existent and independent of man; an outer world that is never fully known. We do not assume that the character of external objects is directly and infallibly mediated through the senses. Indeed, a substantial portion of this book will deal with error, illusion, and self-deception — at the level of perception and cognition and with what we have learned about a man's disposition to error and self-deception in terms of their systematic sources in individual experience, motivation, society, and culture.

We are not, on the other hand, naïve subjectivists persuaded that the external world cannot be known at all, except in a solipsistic construction of reality that bears an unknowable relationship to external objects. Here again a number of chapters will be devoted to an examination of the meaning of subjectivity. We shall show that the traditional emphasis upon exteroceptive input as the sole source of knowledge about reality has left unexplored the little understood inner world and the contribution that interoceptive information makes to man's orientation in the real world. There will be a tension in the book between a conception of reality construction as *colored* — determined by the space-time location of the observer, his rootedness in particular value systems given by his culture and his personal, idiosyncratic life experience — and a conception of man as a seeker after reality as *given*, existent in time, space, matter, energy, and organism and as reflected in the internal consistencies offered by scientific observation of the world.

Science has been enormously successful in providing internally consistent, verified abstractions about the nature of reality and has placed in man's hands increasingly subtle and powerful control over his environment. Science has provided man with a series of cosmological perspectives that have revolutionized man's conceptions of his relation to the universe. This remains an open-ended process. What the future holds we cannot know.

Since the Renaissance, philosophers have been concerned with the specification of the relationship between the phenomena of experience and the material objects in the external world, in an effort to devise an epistemology that provides a rational basis for the pursuits of science. This remains an essentially unsolved problem. The present volume does not presume to make a contribution to the solution of this problem. No explicit epistemological formulations or metaphysical assumptions guide the development of our point of view, except that insofar as we are concerned with the scientific study of perceptual-cognitive processes we are implicitly committed to an assumption of orderliness and lawfulness as an underlying characteristic of the events of consciousness and observable behavior. We are not discussing the nature of a trans-psychological reality that may exist in its own right, except insofar as there may be a true isomorphism between our world of the real and some other world which is reflected in it; but we *are* concerned with the content and form of our reality seeking, and we find that our apprehension of a reality which is real for us constantly goes on growing and becomes more complex, and at the same time, more orderly. It is as if we were nibbling at the edge of a constantly growing reality, pulling something from it into our own little sphere. The world becomes more and more intelligible, in the sense that parts apprehended piecemeal are seen in larger and larger units. Moreover, the very *process* of seeing and understanding becomes, within itself, more and more intelligible. We do not say what this stuff beyond ourselves consists of. We do say, however, that as we continue to approach it, our own conviction increases that there is some sort of ordered relation between the knower and the known.

The title term "encounter" remains unexplained. It is somewhere in semantic space between passivity and activity, between being met and going to meet. We thought at one time of calling this book *The Impulse to Reality* because we wanted to stress the active contact the living organism makes with its world of seeking, selecting, and, beyond it all, invading and carving out for itself a subregion of the world in which it makes its contacts. The word "impulse" also strives to do justice to the tensions, the stresses, the inner-explosive forces by which the life processes within can maintain themselves only by bombarding and capturing energies from without — as when an amoeba sends forth a pseudopod which engulfs and brings within itself a particle of food; and at the same time like the processes by which a beast of prey identifies, strikes down, and incorporates some favorite victim; or when a statesman looks over a region and says, "This is the place," and marks it for settlement. The term "encounter" has been chosen, however, as indicating the vital movement toward active commerce with the environment, a commerce involving reception, utilization, intercommunication, control and the process of being controlled as well; it likewise involves the process by which control and being controlled are shared by the environment as they make their subtle and varying dynamic impact upon the organism. "Encounter" is not limited to embattled knights exchanging mortal thrusts. It comprises also the encounters of love, affiliation, protection; the encounters of exploratory and tentative outreaching and withdrawing.

In the development of the basic themes of this book our approach will be more nearly pluralistic than integrative or synthetic. By placing in dynamic juxtaposition the major insights of many related disciplines — principally those of the psychology of perception and cognition, of learning and neurophysiology, of classical and contemporary psychoanalytic theory, organized around major themes and issues — we shall attempt to develop a coherent and suggestive picture of how man learns to encounter reality, the major processes and determinants of his reality constructions, and much that is unfinished business in his encounter with reality.

Prolegomena

We shall be concerned first with sensory processes and primitive or primary modes of perceptual transformation of the external environment. We shall suggest that the association between sensory functions and "pleasure centers" represents, in man, a primary basis for active contact with the environment, for its active exploration, and active differentiation among phases of the real.

We shall discuss what has been learned about principles underlying the organization of sensory impressions, the dynamic principles of perceptual organization and their neurological bases, which provide in man a patterned and structured vision of reality.

Since learning plays an enormously important role in the

constructions of reality that man develops, great emphasis here
will be given to the conception that learning involves the
learning of perceptual *expectations* and that the learning of
expectation is the learning of *attention*. A guiding view will
be that man structures his environment in terms of the relevance of objects to the achievement of goals.

We shall ask the question: "Do the senses mediate reality?"
and answer it in the negative. We shall show how the process
of scotomatization, as a major barrier to attention, succeeds in
excluding significant segments of reality from recognition
and how the process of reorganization of sensory materials
plays its part in determining perceptual structures. We shall
ask the question: "Is perception a peerless guide to reality?"
and find that reality for the individual emerges out of conflict,
out of conflicting sensory data, out of "dissonant perception";
and that the resolution of such conflict, which makes action
possible, is mediated by principles of inhibition, leading to an
examination of higher levels of personality organization. We
shall see that reality may be conceived of as having psychological meaning, defined in terms of the degrees of compatibility between specific evidence and the broader system of
beliefs that have been set up as a criterion for individual
living.

It is our conviction that the inner world, the internal environment, the so-called subjective world and its contribution to
man's construction of reality, is ready for scientific scrutiny, a
scientific scrutiny that is indeed long overdue. We shall be
concerned here with the role of internal scanning, with the
role of proprioceptive feedback and the proprioceptive system
as a gating system, exercising control over the processing of
exteroceptive input. We shall be interested in the questions of
whether and how the mass of interoceptive sensation can be
brought to conscious awareness and the role that such information may play in the voluntary control of behavior.

We shall draw an image of man not only as constructing
his reality under the pressures of powerful drives, the vicissi-
tudes of personal and life experience, the molding influences of
society and culture, but also as disposed to seek out reality

actively, to reorder and reconstruct in order to gain a clearer and more consistent picture of reality. We shall examine in the final chapters of the book the conditions or factors that are expressive and contributive to this reality-seeking process, the modes by which it is socialized, and the possibilities of strengthening the process through reinforcement.

Finally, we shall raise the question whether man's capacity for reality apprehension must be regarded as limited in principle and in fact — and whether man is justly viewed, in the light of contemporary philosophical pessimism, as alien in an absurd universe. For us, isomorphism — indeed, an isomorphic view of man's relation to the universe as "realistic" — holds out the possibility of reconciliation and the path to the conquest of reality.

2

The Need for Contact

When chemical compounds were formed in the seas of long ago, in such fashion that larger and larger masses could be formed from them, some of the complex end results took on, so to speak, a habit of growing. Some of them, as parts were damaged, replaced the missing parts, and some had a capacity to make copies of themselves. They had, as many biologists have phrased the matter, the capacity for "growth, repair, and reproduction." These are the properties of life as seen in the simplest biological terms.

Typically, such compounds have to be protected by some sort of capsule, membrane, or boundary if they are to withstand the disintegrating effects of the outer world; typically, they involve a perpetual commerce between what is inside and what is outside, as by passage of fluids in one direction or the other. Typically, moreover, what is inside is somewhat unstable. Something is added, or something is taken away, as matter moves in or out, and as chemical "needs" or valences bespeak the readiness of the inside to accept more and more of the outside material. Indeed, with all the instability of the living system, the loss of too much essential material may mean the disintegration of the living thing. We begin to speak then of a *need for oxygen,* brought in and incorporated with what is already there, and a *need for food,* which by chemical reworking will replace portions lost and permit fresh growth. There is not only a need to take in, and a need to repair what has been damaged, but there is a need to extrude that which is irrelevant or interferes with the chemistry of seeking oxygen or seeking food. In the simplest organism there are no specialized organs of acceptance of oxygen or nutriment. There are, however, definite needs, first at the chemical level: then, as we think of the organism as wounded or as threatened by excessive acidity or alkalinity, or as subjected to great pressures or temperatures, we can appropriately say that the *organism is a system of needs,* or we may even say that life is a system of needs.

The living system has often been described in terms of "tensions." They may be very simple, like the surface tensions of droplets within living cells; or, as in the case of a restless youngster who can hardly bear to sit longer in the classroom, we may speak of tension in the muscles, especially the muscles of face, hands, posture, as restlessness passes into squirming, and squirming passes into hyperactivity.

But the term "tension system," useful though it may be, leaves out the problem of *direction.* It suggests too much of the random or chaotic. There is indeed plenty of the chaotic in life, but chaos as observed may be the failure of the observer to know what is happening. Often the movements are almost as unpredictable as are the molecules in a vessel containing a gas. The pressure on the walls of the vessel may seem constant, but this is simply the result of the very large number of molecules constantly bombarding the walls. If there is the slightest leak in the walls of the vessel, there is a concerted movement of the molecules towards the point of the leak. Similarly we may conceive of "tension" in living organisms as issuing in directional movement when there is an unevenness or bias in the "containing" environment.

Now this movement of energies in a progressively more and more specific direction is the first clue to the fact of *impulse,* the first step towards the mobilization of energies towards one rather than another part of the environment, and therefore towards causing one or another kind of result. The concept of a tension system leads to the concept of an impulse system. Impulses are first blind, as in the Freudian *id*. Ontogenetically the organism can first of all be conceived in terms of lack of differentiation between passivity and activity. The first movements, when there is an unevenness in the possibilities for the deployment of energies, are both *passive*, in the sense of being controllable by situations external to the passage of the energies, and *active*, in the sense that the impulses are themselves modes of activity which are effective, insofar as they dominate over the more passive aspects of the environment. The active, by definition, overcomes the passive.

There is probably also here at work a principle which Russian physiologists have called the principle of "dominance," by which any superiority of one contending force over another tends towards accelerated advantage of the stronger over the weaker; compromise fails, the weaker component disappears. Here is the critical point: *The weaker component yields up its energy to the dominant one* (compare page 86). In other words, there is a simplification of life, in the sense that wherever there is a disturbance in the principle of steady tension, whenever there is the beginning of a movement in the direction of the ascendancy of one activity over another, the activity increases in vigor (compare positive feedback, page 62), and the contact which results with the environment is therefore vigorous. As the tension-driven activity gains in vigor, becomes ascendant, and moves towards one rather than another part of the environment, unspecified tensions become discernible as specific impulse.

There are not only "appetitive" activities which seek out, find, assimilate nutrition, and lead on into growth, but there are also activities which lead the growing cell to split and form two cells. At a higher level, such growth takes on the form of asexual and sexual modes of reproduction. There are chemical tendencies which lead towards "warm," "maternal," and variously protective activities that are part of the generative cycle by which the new and small become the old and large. There are also "avoidant" or "aversive" systems, primitive motility permitting movement away from threat or danger.

The Darwinian mechanisms of variation, selection, and survival of the fittest as the basis of adaptation to the environment are appropriate here, as the living system develops its well-defined needs to escape as well as its needs to approach. As regions of safety are found, variation and selection provide mechanisms for advance beyond home base, and withdrawal under appropriate conditions. All these things have to be favorably provided by variation and then selected out through the survival of those organisms which have relatively more of these appropriate ways of meeting such needs, and the elimination of those which have less. Whenever a good fit to a particular corner of the environment is found, there may be a high stabilization for a billion years or more. As the various parts of the world change through cooling, through erosion, through contact of living forms with others they have not previously encountered, each new niche may through appropriate selection give rise to its own new forms of life by a process Simpson has aptly named "adaptive radiation."

NEEDS AND PERCEPTION

Every encounter is a matter of "closing the gap" between some property of the living individual and some property of the environment (or in a few special cases to be noted later, an increase in the magnitude of the gulf of separation). The closing of gaps, so obvious as one pursues prey or mates or things which appeal to the senses, or the increase of gaps as one deals with dangers or aversions, leads to the broader and more metaphorical use of the term "gaps," as one bridges the gap homeostatically between outer temperature and one's own inner temperature, and still more metaphorically, as one bridges the gap between your point of view and ours. Here an especially apposite example is Sokolov's concept of the "orienting response" construed as a process of reducing the gap between a stimulating situation and an existing level. Sokolov and others have shown that as a novel or unanticipated stimulus — a gap in what is known or expected — enters the organism's sphere of awareness, complex inner changes take place. Sensory thresholds are lowered, muscle tone rises, and cortical efficiency and alertness are raised, readying the organism to cope with the challenge of the gap and return to normal levels of arousal when novelty and surprise have been reduced. Helson's generalized formulation of the concept of "adaptation level" is also relevant in this context, in reflecting a general tendency of living individuals to bring inner states and outer conditions into stable concordance.

The biochemical condition of the body — for example, its shortage of sugars — influences its sensitivity for what it needs, as seen immediately at the sensory level. The cruder work of earlier years showed that the need for specific foods could lower the thresholds, that is, make more perceptible even fainter dilutions of the required substances. Yensen induced salt depletion and a mild salt deficiency in human subjects through lowering salt intake and forced excessive sweating. After such "treatment," his subjects reported that low concentrates of sodium chloride, experienced as tasteless prior to treatment, now had a "salty taste."

The more recent and exquisitely detailed work of Pfaffman has shown that solutions requisite to give awareness of taste quality depend upon the biochemical deficits at the time, while Klein's experiments suggest that the need for water after a rich and salty meal, interacting with various cognitive dispositions of the individual, determines what kinds of taste-related objects — sodas, beers, fountains — will be attended to at the time. Freud long ago suggested a biochemical basis for the libido, and Rosenzweig showed nicely that the hormones administered to male subjects determine the multitude of sex responses on the Thematic Apperception Test. Sometimes these biochemical effects are most obvious at the centers, as in the case of various drug effects to be described later (page 96); but such effects appear quite widely in incoming nerve fibers, even in the receptor cells. The whole perceptual response is, to some degree, "loaded" with differential reduction thresholds here and there in terms of biochemical needs.

SENSORY, PERCEPTUAL, AND COGNITIVE NEEDS

There appear to be many kinds of needs for specific types of stimulation. Sometimes the stimulation is related to vital visceral need; sometimes it is apparently just sensory stimulation in its own right. In the healthy and "sated" organism, there may be a need for exteroceptive stimulation. There may be a need for sensory "nutriment" of some sort, and distress resulting from deprivation of the usual incoming sensory stimulation. One may speak of the need for such stimulation as cognate with the need for ordinary food nutriment. Moreover, needs are more complex than they seem. Thus need for water would depend upon the drying of the mucous membranes of the mouth and throat; but there may also be delight in the cold water of a spring, beyond the point of satiation. There may be need for "coldness" in the warm membranes. There may also be a perseverative need; one starts drinking and goes on drinking. And there may be a stress need for activity (compare page 12). There seems to be a need for color and tone after long periods of monotonous and limited environmental stimulation; and there may indeed be a general level of sensory need, just as there is a need for a general level of activity. Complete lack of sensory input might be as disturbing as a complete inactivity, and as tension-arousing, and such lack may be conducive to activity which results in exposure of sensory surfaces to the environment.

This introduces the problem of *curiosity*, to which a great deal of excellent research has been directed in the last few years. Curiosity may be conceived as a need for the new, or the complex, or both. Thus Smock and Holt have shown that children with high curiosity seek, when free to do so, relatively complex stimulus patterns to attend to, as contrasted with those low on the curiosity dimension. This is reminiscent of the time-honored conception of "progressive mastery," by which we get deeper and deeper into the complex integrations characteristic of the arts or sciences. Thus H. T. Moore found that complex chords, too hard to hear as chords, became more satisfying for practiced listeners, while simpler chords became boring.

It might be suggested that the term "curiosity" is doing too many kinds of work. There is certainly the primitive satisfaction in a stimulus near the adaptation level, and related to some primitive pleasure, as in lying on a gently warming afternoon, half-dozing in the sunshine, or listening to very light and casual dinner music, or just plain relaxing as relaxing. Some of these, notably the last, sound as if pleasure from movement away from tension or conflict were the central essence; but as we see man avidly immersing himself in the environment, surely a place must be found for our hammering at the doors of greater and greater challenges, complexities, or difficulties.

Moreover, the active process of *seeking*, whether one finds or not, can be satisfying, perhaps for a wide variety of reasons, some arising from past reinforcement and some from the participation of a muscular component, as one chases the stimulus. This is probably related to a principle well used by Woodworth, who speaks of "perceptual drives," and of self-reinforcing acts of perceiving. This may be generalized very broadly in terms of a theory that goes back to Aristotle to the effect that there is a "need" to *use* whatever equipment one possesses. It has been well stated in modern terms by Karl Bühler. He speaks of "function pleasure": very simply, man gets gratification from using whatever he has. Certainly the sensory functions come under this head, as do the perceptual functions at a slightly higher level at which there is a combination of sensory components into a new unit. Beyond these, there is, of course, the mastery of the function itself, and the mastery of the environment, perhaps also mastery of the self; the removal of uncertainties and anxieties; and a host of subtle, but important factors relating to the creation of order. Several of these factors will be examined later. Probably they interact, reinforce one another, build themselves into complex architectures.

THE INNER ENVIRONMENT AS A MINIATURE OF THE OUTER

Since life arose in the sea, the physical and chemical properties of living organisms had first to be very much like the properties of the sea itself. The "normal saline" used by the surgeon reflects the fact that the body is salty. The bony structure, even the nervous system, of creatures which have lived for eons as air breathers on the surface of the earth can be traced back to the salt water conditions surrounding their early ancestry. The biochemist confronts an amazing variety of inner changes in the form of metabolism of protein, carbohydrate, and fat, which may be conceived as a chain of chemical events leading back again ultimately to commerce with the chemistry of the environment. The contraction of muscle must obey, indeed, must mimic, the general mechanical realities of the nonliving world. Levers of Types 1, 2, and 3, as known to the physicist, do their exquisite work in the movements of arms and legs. The physics of reflection and refraction of light appear in the impacts of light upon cornea and lens.

The patterning of the inner upon the model of the outer goes far indeed. Polyak showed with great subtlety that the visual centers in the brain, in which specialized visual impressions record the outer environment, are laid out in a geometrical scheme essentially conformable to the way in which the retina is structured. Despite all the complex sorting and regrouping of the pathways in the nervous system by which the messages from the body surface get to the brain, there are still, within the brain, regions corresponding to broad classes of sense organ activity. There are, for example, visual, auditory, and other regions in the cerebral cortex. It appears from Penfield's work that there is even some "fine" localization of memories. The patient under local anesthesia for a brain operation is electrically stimulated at a specific point, and this *point*, when stimulated, may consistently bring back the same memory. We cannot yet say just how accurate and precise and constant such localization is. But it indicates a general or orderly correspondence of the inner organization to the outer organization represented by the environment.

There are, indeed, three forms of organization, each of which is related to the other two. (1) There is the organization of the environment as a whole, in terms of its distribution of objects which can make their impression on us through one sensory function or another. (2) There is the more or less comparable organization of the receiving and acting system within the body. (3) There is the inner, representational organization, or world of the personal, the world of three-dimensional space, as mediated by eye, ear, and touch, subjectively laid out, which has enough conformity to the outer world to permit us to drive a car or read a book. Each of these three systems, "isomorphic" with the others — that is, having "*equal* (or *comparable*) form" with the others — is in a state of continuous change, and there is therefore some flexibility, some modulation or resonance of one to the other. (Cf. Sokolov, above, page 14.)

There are, of course, perfectly definite limits to the capacity of the organism to take over the pattern of the environment. Despite much flexibility, there are life processes of very high stability. Some of these will be of special importance in our task here. For example, some of the chemical compounds that were formed quite early in the history of life have set a pattern fundamental for heredity. They cannot yield; they cannot budge; and if they are disturbed, the organism dies. Speaking in terms of species or of strain or of family resemblance, we encounter the exquisite detail with which the nucleotides are put together in the DNA-RNA pattern of genetics, representing a delicate but persisting structure which, put down in temporal and spatial order, provides the pattern of each new life. There is, so to speak, a chemical axis as real as — and indeed more fundamental than — the bony structure of the skeleton we think of as determining the structural system of the growing individual. The actual structural center and core of the life process can be conceived in biochemical terms, in terms of the systematic time-space interrelationships among chemical processes, often of a very high order of complexity.

3

Primary Modes of Encounter

Since the cells of the body are all derivative, as we saw, from the conditions prevailing in the environment, notably, its chemical basis and its chemical possibilities, it is hardly surprising that the cells are never fully differentiated chemically from their surround, nor from one another. It is in keeping with our conception of the evolutionary process that there is much isomorphism between what goes on inside and what goes on outside, and that there is much mutual selectivity in terms of similarities, and sometimes in terms of contrasts. It is the very nature of enzymes, which appear early in the staging from which life appears, to regulate the flow of substances and to assist in the creation of new chemical compounds. From this vantage point, there is nothing surprising about the fact that the sensory cells are attuned to the world beyond the organism, and that they serve to bring the environment into a pervading relationship with the organism; what we call sensory drives are nothing other than the active processes by which compounds within living cells move out towards the environment and bring it back into the cells. In fact, in the light of work such as Pfaffman's, we know the details of this process in the case of the chemoreceptors.

But it is not only *substances* which are brought in; it is process, especially rhythmic process. As E. B. Holt showed long ago, it is the nature of sight and hearing to bring into the organism those periodicities, those wave lengths which are active in the environment. A sympathetic vibration is set up, as in the Helmholtz theory of hearing. There is photic driving, the resonance of the central nervous system itself to the vibration rates imposed by the periodicity of a flashing light.

SENSORY FUNCTIONS AND PLEASURE

But the organism does not passively await such stimulation. It is highly selective, for both substances and processes whose rhythms are in accord with its own. It is provided with equipment which scans, catches, and sweeps into the interior what it needs.

What is this equipment? Partly it is the nervous system as a whole whose rhythms, whose sensitivities welcome some kinds of "input" and reject other kinds. Indeed, the principle of "function pleasure" would necessarily mean that all energies would be welcome which stimulated or facilitated normal function. But there is much specialization of organs, tissues, and individual cells.

We have learned in recent years that the brain stem contains regions whose excitation is intimately related to the life of affect, emotion, and feeling, in a broad sense. Through the research of the last two decades and especially that of Delgado and Olds it has become clear that the affect or feeling life of higher animals is to some degree localizable in specific, differentiated structures within the brain stem. By implanting electrodes in the desired region, it is possible to touch what have been called "pleasure centers." A rat thus implanted may, by pressing a bar or by some other appropriate movement, send a current into the electrode and therefore stimulate a specific region in his own brain. Sometimes he does this very rapidly with almost frantic repetitive effort. He acts as if he were doing this because he wanted to. When the electrode is shifted to other regions, the behavior tapers off, or may stop dead. (There are regions which are now thought to be centers for unpleasantness or distress in the sense that the animal will not activate them when he is free to do so.) As the animal will ordinarily work for a specific reward, which must act upon his sense organs and send a message to his brain, so he may *short-cut* this process and get the direct effect on his brain without "needing" the outer stimulus. Man can artificially contrive a quick and easy pleasure; the animal, under natural conditions, has to bring the environment into his body by a much longer, more complicated process. But bringing the environment in is what the whole system is contrived to do. In general, whatever kinds of reward the animal will work for, in terms of food, water, mates, etc., may be conceived to be normal stimulators through the incoming pathways of the specific pleasure regions. He directly activates the appropriate pleasure center, each one of which seems to be rather well differentiated from others.

It has long been known that various types of central nervous system injuries, lesions, and post-febrile disease produce dramatic disorders in the feeling life of some patients. There is some little work from higher animals and a tiny fragment of work from human subjects which seem to indicate that this localization of pleasure centers is a broad mammalian attribute, just as is the relative localization of sensory functions.

The relevance of all this for our theme regarding sensory gratification is twofold. On the one hand, it is now likely that the gratifications from sensory stimulation are not based primarily upon cortical activity in the projection areas, but rather upon their connections with the pleasure centers. Pleasures, in other words, have their sensory sources, as everyday observation has always suggested. On the other hand, in the long slow process of differentiation so characteristic of evolution, organisms have been selected, and have survived, in which pleasures, positively oriented responses, have arisen in conjunction with biologically needed responses. Concentrated specialized regions have gradually taken over specific functions related to the world of individual experience, in the case of affect, as in the case of the sensory processes.

Even before the learning process complicates the matter, then, there are associations between certain sense functions and certain pleasures: these relations appear early in mammalian development, and constitute an important basis for active contact with the environment, active exploration, active differentiation between different phases of the real.

Seeking and Scanning

The process of growth of the central nervous system involves much more than increase in size, and more than relatively greater increases in size of one region over another. There is also active differentiation even when size remains constant; that is, there is greater and greater specialization in a particular region. The differentiation shows up functionally in the sense that various reflexes appear which could not appear before differentiated structures, upon which they depend, were available. Differentiation is also biochemical, as for example, in the development of certain endocrine organs to produce not only one, but several different kinds of endocrine substances. The term "maturation" is ordinarily used to mean increased specificity of structure and function within the central nervous system. But the differentiation of sensory cells within the sense organ is likewise a form of maturation, as is the development of the structures within the autonomic nervous system. Maturation makes sense organs more and more capable of differentiated response to a differentiated stimulus world. Motor components such as the external eye muscles, and the muscles involved in turning, reaching, withdrawing, etc., also involve progressive enrichment of the contact-making equipment.

This mobility of the equipment which carries the sense organs is of vast importance for the discovery of the reality which lies outside. It is, in fact, a primary source for gathering information, as the sensory surfaces are moved and brought into exposure with various kinds of specialized energies — light, sound, warmth, floating particles — upon which we depend for orientation to the world. In its most primitive form, this movement of the sense organs occurs reflexively, about as soon as the sense organs and their supporting equipment exist. If you once allow variation in the sensory input, you will probably soon find yourself involved in the world of comparison, the primitive capacity for judgment, analogy, and if any memory impressions are left, the basis also for time perspective, and soon for anticipation of the future. The diversification of sensory impressions, so slight as long as the organism remains stationary, become richly elaborated as this primitive process of moving and carrying the receptors appears.

Here we must introduce the terms "seeking" and "scanning." The first such activities appear to be utterly blind and without explicit purpose. There is only that purpose which lies in the evolutionary background, in the sense that those organisms have been selected for life in which there are the restless impulsive movements of these structures. As these structures move and contacts are made which lead into pleasure centers, we imagine some primitive learning process to begin, and soon a goal-directed or purposive act to follow. English usage seems to permit using the term "seeking" only when there is a specific goal; let us restrict the term "scanning" to the first blind activities, but then as goals associated with pleasure are identified, let us refer to organized "seeking." Such seeking will involve selecting among contingent possibilities, among all the things that have gratifying qualities. Since two or more of these qualities may compete for the control of the organism, there must be some *exclusion* as well as *inclusion* in the processes of scanning and seeking.

THE PROCESS OF ATTENDING

Here we need to consider the process of *attending*. In its primitive form, this is conceived as a response which brings the sensory surfaces into increasingly good contact with those cues that have activated the process of scanning and seeking (Holt). The process of cue utilization continues, and becomes more efficient as scanning and seeking proceed; there are soon *habits of attending*, drawing the cue object into the center of the perceptual field, such as the fovea, or the tip of the tongue, or the tips of the fingers, in which richer differentiation is possible. After the object is secured in such a differentiated region, it may be either held or given up. Indeed, there is experimental evidence that attention, in this sense of scanning and seeking, is a process quite different from that which is involved in holding what has once been found. The process of holding or fixating is related to Freud's idea of "attention cathexis," that is, the binding or progressive fixation of the organism in such a manner as to make it reach or hold more and more of a given kind of stimulation. The following account by Gesell of the development of visual "regards" in the human infant exemplifies both the emergence of "holding" and the growth of patterns of scanning and seeking. According to Gesell, *et al.*:

At 1 week the baby stares without fixation
4–12 weeks: looks at mother's face, adults' hands and own hands; face brightens
6 weeks: starey gaze, true inspection, follows retreating figure of mother, a moment of searching, more alert, adaptive
16 weeks: protracted moment of staring, knows mother, sobers when he sees strangers
24 weeks: recurrence of regard
28 weeks: perceptual behavior; interest in own abilities, can be content alone, concentrates on an object
40–52 weeks: inquisitive visual and motor behavior; intent on regarding what other person does; perceptive moods, gives and takes
52–56 weeks: imitates

IMPRINTING AND CANALIZATION

So far we have regarded the process of sensing and also the process of attending as forms of perception in which the environment is, in a fairly literal sense, transported into the organism. A concept widely used in the study of the learning process here stands up and demands our attention: the process of imprinting. In its German origin, and in its English use, the term suggests that something has been brought from outside, and pressed upon or into the tissues of the organism. The Roman poet, Catullus, noted that the little pet sparrow made sexual advances to the hand which fed and petted it. The American experimentalist, Wallace Craig, observed similar modulations of sexual, and of feeding and nest-building responses, in birds to which the "appropriate" object was not, at the time, available. The response may be made, so to speak, by analogy. For example, birds will build nests with strips of paper if they have no twigs at hand.

The question thus arises: will they "learn to accept" this not quite "adequate" stimulus? Of course, the answer is that sometimes they will, and sometimes they will not. Perhaps the heart of the problem lies in the question of whether one can so impress a particular stimulus upon an animal or bird, that it will act "as if" the object were "adequate." We have to use a good many quotation marks here, and we become a little disturbed as to what we mean by *adequate, familiar, appropriate,* and so on. The plot thickens, and we find ourselves dealing with the general question: "If there is a broad class of stimuli capable of eliciting a given instinctual response, and some object, which is not at the center or region of greatest valence, but off towards the edge, is used, can it come to acquire a central position, as if it had been the most preferred stimulus in the first place?"

In this context we introduce the celebrated instances, so well described and photographically rendered by Konrad Lorenz. Noting how the fledgling greylag gosling follows its mother, he strides forth in advance of a gosling which has no experience with a mother to follow, and becomes a "mother" for all subsequent *following* purposes. So now, the critical issue stands out: Will the gosling now follow its mother as well? The answer appears to be "no." What has happened is that a nonpreferred moving object, such as the human being, has not only come into the center of the band of stimulating possibilities, but has taken over the function served by the whole prior band; the fledgling apparently will follow no other exemplar of the band, at least as long as the central one upon which practice has been obtained is available.

Hess and his followers and collaborators have used a decoy going round and round in a track quacking, and verified the proneness of these birds to follow whatever becomes the initial model. Moreover, by making it *harder* (trotting up hill), or by involving more effort than is necessary in other cases, they have shown that effort is apparently a factor which stamps in the response more firmly.

Imprinting processes are not confined to birds. Scott appears to have shown that the acquisition of social tendencies in puppies is based at least in part upon "imprinting-like learning," that is, upon exposure to particular social objects very early in life. Similarly Harlow's work with monkeys suggests imprinting-like learning as the young monkey develops attachments to mother or mother surrogates through familiarity, becoming more exclusive with time.

The imprinting process is a little like the old law of "prior entry" which indicates that among two or more competing stimuli, that which hits the organism first has the more intense effect. We may be dealing with some primitive principle of "primacy," in which the first object of a class relevant to a need becomes firmly built in. Later, from a reflective viewpoint, that object seems more appropriate. It is like F. H. Lund's "law of primacy in persuasion." "Old friends are the dearest." If one could hold constant the age and maturation level of different living individuals of a given species, one could probably say that the first things with which they have experience probably have the right of way over other things of the same class. It is generally thought that many of these imprinted responses are fixed for life. They are said not to extinguish.

Processes of this general type have been described under the term "canalization," chiefly emphasizing instances of early gratification of needs of various sorts in infancy and childhood, and suggesting that these often get built into permanent personality structure, being very resistive to extinction, and in many ways, quite unlike any types of conditioning of which we now have knowledge. Canalization is conceived as another case in which the structure of the environment, both its temporal and spatial structure, is built *within the person*. Surely a firmly ingrained habit system which involves gratifications in a given sequence is quite different from a conditioned habit system, which can be extinguished if no longer reinforced.

Assimilation and Accommodation

However, the analysis by Piaget has underscored another developmental pattern. He distinguishes between *assimilating* — bringing the properties of the environment into the mental structures of the subject — and *accommodating* — altering the properties of the observing subject to make them similar in quality or structure to those of the stimulating environment. Both these processes are evidently related to Sokolov's gap-closing process mentioned above (page 14) and to Helson's conceptions of adaptation level. They are conveniently stressed at this point because they emphasize the progressive adaptation of inner and outer processes to one another, and serve to bring out the nature of the compromise which always exists between organism and environment in the immediate region of the organism's shell, skin, or capsule, a process which emphasizes the absence of any absolute line of separation between the one and the other.

It has also been possible for Piaget in this frame of reference to define the manner in which a particular portion of the stimulus world, or indeed of any small stimulus object, is held or attended to, with relative exclusion or belittlement of other parts of the stimulating situation. This, according to his theory and observations, should cause an actual intensification of the subjective impact, making a stimulus appear bigger, brighter, more vivid when fixated, and quantitative evidence should be able to define that his process of "centration" is actually a source of perceptual changes of a lawful sort. For example, in the case of size estimation of an experimentally varied stimulus and a standard stimulus, both in the visual field at the same time, the standard would be expected to receive much more centration because one keeps looking back and forth, using the standard more than any one comparison stimulus. The "error of the standard" (overestimation of the standard stimulus) which thus results is a familiar laboratory finding. Such observations confirm our view that the process of perceiving is never a simple matter of registry upon a sensory or a central process. It initiates complex adaptive responses, and since the adaptive responses vary, the stimulus is received in varying guise. The world is transformed by the very process of observing it.

However, the world is continually being sought, and to say that it is greatly "transformed" as a datum for our experience is not in itself evidence that the ultimate, objective reality — whatever that may be, the "thing in itself" to which Kant alludes — is itself transformed. That issue will be a later chapter in our story (page 83). Here it is sufficient to say that confrontation of the environment is never a photographic plate process, but always a selecting, excluding, rearranging, and modulating process.

4

Outer Structure Becomes
Inner Structure

We have already assumed that sensory processes get connected one with another. Indeed, we connect things "by contiguity," as the factory whistle is connected with the sound of machinery at 7 o'clock, or the classroom bell is connected with the hushing of conversation and the beginning of the lecture, as January is connected with snow for the Adirondack dweller, and summer sports for the New Zealander. Peer at the brain and note the rich connections of the cells from different cortical sensory projection areas, and the damage or interference with associations as some portions of the brain suffer lesions. Ascending and descending paths are supplemented by transcortical tracts of many sorts. It is not a wild assumption to say that the activation of one sensory region can give rise to the activation of another, and that this can serve as the basis for ordinary, everyday association of sensory impressions, or of sense impressions, with the warmed-over or trace impressions from earlier experience, as postulated by the association psychology from the time of David Hartley, 1749, on to the present.

These phenomena are brought into relation to modern learning theory by Kenneth Spence, in terms of the concept of "SS" learning. In SS learning we do not assume the proprioceptive feedback effects of movement arriving in the brain's cortical projection centers in order to get learning; i.e., learning may represent a process of direct connection-forming between the sensory impressions themselves, or between sense impressions and their deposits or residues, their traces or "images." These will interact with one another, and with new incoming stimuli as if all were in terms of fresh sensory stimulation, exactly as presupposed by David Hartley.

Most charming, and in some ways, most simple and direct is the doctrine of the French essayist, Condillac, who asked us to imagine a statue endowed with exactly one psychological function, and no other; namely, the sense of smell. Give it no memory, no imagination, no ego.

> If we give the statue a rose to smell, to us it is a statue smelling a rose, to itself it is smell of rose . . . but our statue has yet no idea of the different changes it can undergo. Thus it is well without wishing to be better, or ill without wishing to be well. Suffering can no more make it desire a good it does not know than enjoyment can make it fear an ill it does not know. . . . It exists, then, without being able to form desires.

Sensations later become connected not only with one another, but with desire; for odors are pleasant or unpleasant, and there is desire and ultimately action towards the acquisition of those sensations with which pleasure is associated (compare pages 21–23). This cheerful whimsy, like many such first beginnings in a philosophic mining expedition, finally strikes pay dirt.

A more complex system dealing with the same ideas was developed in the early nineteenth century by J. F. Herbart, who believed that sense impressions compete with one another for a place in consciousness; that such impressions, even after lapsing from consciousness into an unconscious realm, continue to compete with one another; that their competition and conflict result in the relative success of some in pushing their way back into consciousness, the relative failure of others to do so. Finally, we reach the conception that any new impression of any sort can find a place in consciousness insofar as there is an organized world of impressions ready to assimilate it, an "apperception mass." The SS conceptions of today need, of course, to be considered in the light of this dynamic background, this conception of the intrinsic relations of sensation as *competitive*, rather than limited to possibilities for connection, for coupling and uncoupling.

Herbart's conception gives us an organized world of experience, some of it in consciousness at the time, some of it stored or organized beneath the threshold of consciousness, ready, so to speak, like a pitcher plant, to trap whatever relevant thing comes its way. Similar and richer dynamic conceptions have developed among evolutionary biologists.

There is, from an evolutionary point of view, "species space" like that of von Uexküll's space in which the tick apprehends the odors and touch qualities which invite him to dig into the skin of his host, rejecting all that smells or feels wrong or irrelevant to his need. At the smell of butyric acid emanating from the animal passing beneath, it drops; and if the surface qualities are right, it burrows in.

Similarly, by detailed analysis of visual receptors and known differentiating capacities, von Uexküll describes the perceptual space within which insects, mammals, and human beings select, reject, and organize what is meaningful to them.

Psychologists, in conceptualizing the process whereby new impressions are integrated or coordinated with pre-existing apperceptive structures, have undertaken to show that a *structured space* — the "behavioral environment" of Koffka, or the "personal space" of William Stern — characterizes this function. The processes involved are thought to have organized, dynamic properties in terms of which new impressions are assimilated or rejected and which in effect impose upon the environment their intrinsic "demands."

There is not only species space, but also individual space. Thus, for example, in accordance with Stern's "personal space" principles, the space of the left-handed and the right-handed man should be measurably different, having their own curvatures and distorting qualities. McNamara and Fisch found that illusions in the right half of the visual field of the right-handed person corresponded to those in the left half of the visual field of the left-handed person. They describe their findings in the following terms:

> In a depth perception task, when all cues (except size) were excluded, there was a significant tendency for right-handed subjects to place the object on the right behind the one on the left, and vice versa for left-handers, regardless of whether the left or right stimulus was used as the "Standard." We conclude that laterality contributes to the "error of the standard" effect. This is thought to occur through the fixation of attention toward the preferred side, i.e., left or right directions in space.

Here the world of the right-hander has probably imposed, in addition, special perceptual difficulties upon left-handers, and the world of eyes and legs complicates the matter.

The foregoing strongly implies that the "natural order," represented to us by geography and by science, is less uniform, person for person, at the perceptual level than it is at the conceptual or abstract level. Indeed, Piaget's researches on the development of the understanding of elementary geometry support such a contention. This does not mean caprice and whim — arbitrary, personal, or subjective shaping of the experienced world. It means simply that there is an interaction between the constitutional sensory and associative capacities of the individual (the general spatial-temporal realities which all must face) and the special cultural emphases and requirements, together with family and community requirements, which give a distinctive personal note to the structuring process.

But it is time to look a little more closely at the functions of the central nervous system in relation to this whole reality-apprehending process. In his monumental *Integrative Action of the Nervous System,* Sir Charles Sherrington defined the process of sensory input in terms of three coordinated systems: the exteroceptive system mediating contact with the outer environment; the interoceptive system, conveying messages from the internal world of mucous membranes, vital organs, and scattered receptors through all the living tissues; and proprioceptors, carrying information from the striped muscles, tendons, and joints, as changes in relative position of the limbs, neck, and trunk, and the musculature are effected. It was clear to him that one discovers and makes use of internal information just as one makes use of external information. The axis of reference, consisting of the central nervous system, is neither in nor out; it stands, as it were, at the center, receiving from domestic and foreign delegates, on equal terms, and binding the three groups of messages into an integrated communication and diplomatic system, in which appropriate action is controlled in terms of all three kinds of information. The nervous system may sum the impressions, as from many scattered spots on the surface, to which a very small quantity of acid is applied; one will not produce reaction, but the sum may do so. There may likewise be temporal summation: no reflex is elicited by a first stimulus, but after *successive* stimulation at the same point it appears. There is also much integration of separate pathways as they converge upon a "final common path," and there is much dominance of one reflex system over another — a response to pain, for example, has the right of way over a normally expectable locomotor or extensor thrust response.

Therefore, one may say that even when stimulation is applied to the passive animal, a very complex process of selection from incoming messages is going on. There is selection at the receptor level as well as at the effector level. There is, in other words, patterning of the input from the world, as there is in the response to it. In this case the structure of the central nervous system works conjointly with the structure of the stimulus pattern imposed upon it (compare photic driving, page 21). Since Sherrington's time, much attention has also been given to the fact that the order imposed upon both perceptual and motor systems is often given by the highest centers of the cerebral cortex (compare the discussion of inhibition, page 85).

Another instance of patterning, so well suggested by these earlier studies, was explicitly investigated by Gibson, and by Gibson and Walk, who have made much of stimulus texture in relation to the possibilities of high-level interpretation, as in the "visual cliff" shown in Figure 1. It also now appears that the structure in the stimulus world is a fundamental part of the normal process of maintaining an orientation to it; stimulus deprivation seems to do its work not through lack of specific elements, but through lack of the usual patterning, and therefore, the attention values and meanings of the stimulus world. Patterning, such as Gibson's, may very well be related to sensory deprivations as studied by René Spitz, who observed that many infants lacking in social stimulation fell behind in basic adaptive skills.

But the world acting upon us consists of a pattern, many components of which do not break into the field of awareness. The world apprehended is a world of relevance to the individual's needs at the time; even when one has no *reportable* impression at all regarding the stimulus acting at the time, one makes an appropriate perceptual, and indeed an appropriate affective response to it. Philip Holzman's studies of autonomic nervous system response to voices show "physiological turbulence" even when one does not *recognize* that the voice is one's own, and Donald Spence's studies indicate that the threshold of relevance, so to speak, is different from the threshold of reportability. This could have been suspected by noting the mother who can sleep through the circus calliope, but awakens at the infant's change in breathing, or the classical instance of the miller who awakens not from the noise of the mill, but when his mill stops.

Our purpose so far has been to show that the perceiving organism is not a helpless, passive victim flooded by sensory

Figure 1. Though supported by heavy plate glass, the kitten has stopped its forward progress and turned left. The texture of visual cues from the checkerboard under the glass denotes a sharp drop just ahead.

stimuli, who stores sensory impressions helter-skelter in memoric bins. Rather, he is more appropriately conceived to accept or reject, assimilate or extrude sensory stimulation in accordance with principles that suggest a structured organized process, based partly upon the limiting possibilities and opportunities for integration of sensory messages in the central nervous system, and partly upon a complex and prolonged process of learning. Emphasis in this chapter has been upon some conceptions that have been advanced as to the nature of the principles that underlie these organizing, structuring processes. Thus we have spoken of species space and personal space, of apperception mass and pattern perception. We have suggested that the structuring process is dynamic, and we turn next to the contribution that learning and experience make to the development of the structured perceptual world of reality.

But before we go on to an extended discussion of the processes whereby inner structure is developed and elaborated, it behooves us to clarify the meaning of the conception of *structure* itself. In doing so, we owe a considerable debt to H. A. Murray's critical analysis of this concept, evolved over a lifetime of thought. Here we strive to paraphrase and condense his suggestions:

In the external environment we find things arranged in space and time with more or less predictable or stable relations to one another in these dimensions. Things in the external environment, their spatial and temporal relations, have a relevance for our needs as living organisms — they serve functions. We shall see in the next chapter that much of learning is the learning of *expectations* predicated upon the space-time arrangements of things in the outer world as related to our needs. When we speak now of inner structure, we refer to *recurrent* and *predictable organizations of behavior* — perceptual and cognitive — which reflect in some measure the way things are organized in the outer world of space and time. But here we must give particular emphasis to the temporal dimension of inner structure: it is structure in the sense that organized, integrated patterns of behavior recur in time, and, given a knowledge of the environmental circumstances, are predictable. This conception of inner structure gives too little emphasis to flexibility, change, and growth. Inner structure is never immutably fixed or frozen, and though it may achieve a high degree of stability, even evanescent patterns of behavior may be highly integrated, though short-lived in a changing, "temporal procession" of adaptive behavior.

5

Learning, Attending, and the Real

We have attempted to indicate that there is some value in the concept of "reality," even without consideration of the learning of words and other symbols. There is at least some differentiation evident in terms of the quality of the things human beings encounter. There is differentiation in terms of events humans locate within and events experienced as outside. There is differentiation by virtue of grouping together systems of external events which are subject to change as the result of extraorganic forces and are contrasted with a system of internal events which appear, to some degree, independent of such pressures from outside. So, if by "real" one means that which is relatively stable, then the inner will be more real; if one means that which is less dependent upon the organism's inner structure, then by definition the external will be more real.

Actually, we are not quite ready for consideration of the criteria of the real because no account has been taken of our *success* or *failure* to encounter the expected. There are no "false positives" here; the problem of the real arises only when expectations are falsified. The process of *expecting* is an important fundamental in the definition of the real. Now the learning process results in *expectation;* it readies us to expect things, some of which happen and some of which do not happen. It is therefore to the learning process, as it prepares humans for such readiness or expectation, that we must now turn.

CLASSICAL CONDITIONING AND THE LEARNING OF EXPECTATIONS

Though beginning with a starkly objective, physiological approach, the Pavlov type of conditioned response, now called "classical," early came to be understood as a form of "anticipatory response." In the Soviet psychology of recent years Anokhin's analysis has broadly justified the view that the conditioned response is a preparation for the unconditioned stimulus, a process of readiness which has a definite time course, and moves towards fuller readiness as time passes; then, with failure to receive the impact of the unconditioned stimulus, the response may wane.

Thus Zener, describing a motion picture record of the total behavior of a dog, conditioned to salivate at the sounding of a bell, writes that the reaction of the dog is: ". . . describable as a looking for, expecting the fall of the food with a readiness to perform the eating behavior which will occur when the food falls." Here, then, is the beginning of a kind of reality anticipation which, defined in rudimentary fashion by physiological preparation for a situation, succeeds or fails. One begins to take note of the phenomenon of anticipation, and with it, the rudimentary beginnings of a time awareness. When the expectation is fulfilled by the physiological reality of the expected impact, there is the rudimentary beginning of a conception of the real, as contrasted with the unreal. The generalization of the conditioned response would, from this point of view, be the arousal of a broadened expectancy so that a stimulus similar to the familiar conditioned stimulus produces the habitual response to some observable degree, and the extinction of the response would be the progressive reduction or disappearance of the conditioned (anticipatory) response.

This is the beginning of "attention." The first stages in this process belong to "involuntary attention" — aroused by suddenness, intensity, or massiveness, ultimately probably figure-ground or dominance qualities of the stimulus — which commands both general activation and specific responses whose thresholds for the stimulus are low. But there is also the process of "voluntary attention," based upon "learning to attend," a very complex process indeed. Some of it is primitive conditioning, but in its full form it is far beyond our present powers of analysis.

OPERANT CONDITIONING AND THE LEARNING OF ATTENTION

In accordance with current usage, we may distinguish the Pavlov type of conditioning from operant conditioning; operant behavior embodies repetition of acts not arising experimentally, but spontaneously associated with reinforcements or rewards. There seems to be a good deal of evidence that gratification of needs, sometimes appearing in the form of tension reduction and occasionally tension increase, is the central fact about reinforcement. As Thorndike used to say, "Wait until the organism does what you want it to do and then reward it." There is also a fair amount of evidence to suggest that it is through communication with the pleasure centers, exactly as in classical association theory (compare page 30 above), that adventitious stimuli take over the capacity to produce such repetition of certain acts. There are, in other words, secondary as well as primary reinforcers. It is not only the candy in the mouth, but the "Yes, you may" to the "child expecting reward" that acts to guide behavior. From the present viewpoint and in terms of the necessities of experimental procedure, we cannot ordinarily define what initiates the behavior, but we can say that under certain conditions it is more likely to occur.

When it occurs, you can reward it, and from that point on it will occur more frequently or more vigorously, or with longer duration, or in some other way such that it can be said to be "strengthened."

As concepts of operant conditioning developed side by side with concepts of perceptual differentiation and perceptual learning, it became clear that many acts of attending would have to be viewed as operants which might be highly relevant to problems of seeking and scanning, problems of figure-ground organization, problems of selection and exclusion, and ultimately problems of perceptual structure and dynamics. Why not bring together the conditioning of *overt* acts and the conditioning of certain *inner* acts, whatever they may be, to which the term "attending" is applied? It would be simple and useful if it should turn out that some acts of attending are operants obeying all the laws found for motor operants, especially if it should also turn out to be true that miniature inner events, such as movement of the eyes or of internal eye muscles as well as external or the micromusculature connected with the hearing process, or the touching, grasping, reaching activities of the fingers, hands, and arms, are all subject to laws of operant conditioning. From such a viewpoint we might set up a hypothesis that operant conditioning of acts of attending is a major clue to the definition of perceptual structure, and, more broadly, towards the differentiation of an anticipated from an unanticipated, a true-to-expectations versus a false-to-expectations kind of a world. At this level the world of the real might be defined in terms of attending processes.

THE LEARNING OF SYMBOLS AND THE STRUCTURE OF REALITY

It is highly probable, as much Soviet work on conditioning suggests, that there is a genuine difference in levels between the rather mechanical early Pavlovian conditioned responses, and those later responses based upon organized linguistic cues, that is, upon symbols. Razran has produced elaborate evidence that in vertebrates through and including the level of the fishes, there is simple and rather mechanical Pavlovian conditioning, and that above this level there are symbolic responses subject to somewhat different formal principles. (Pavlov early distinguished between a primary signal system in which a previously indifferent stimulus becomes a signal for the unconditioned stimulus, and a secondary signal system, denoting the role of words in conditioning as that of "signals of signals.")

In the study of human infants and children it appears to be clear that for about the first year and a half in the normal infant we are dealing largely with simple Pavlovian conditioned reflexes, but, above that, with linguistic structures of higher complexity, involving somewhat different laws. Such laws relate to different principles of extinction; the verbal does not extinguish as fast as the preverbal conditioned response.

We might say then that reality appears in primitive form at the level of the first signal system, but that a new kind of reality emerges as the symbol world develops. The real is now more than just what is *expected;* it is that which has been expectantly *named,* especially that which has been expectantly named by oneself. You can name it *into* existence and name it *out* of existence. Words help to define the world in which one anticipates events and is confirmed or frustrated with regard to anticipations. (Even a shocking failure to experience the expected can often be renamed and rationalized.) This could be called Reality Type Number 2, as contrasted with the primitive sensory anticipation factors which we could call Reality Type Number 1.

Indeed, Benjamin Lee Whorf has suggested that language plays a major role in dissecting and organizing the world of the real. The Whorf-Sapir hypothesis asserts that language does not merely reflect cognitive organization of reality, but that the meaning and process categories of language help determine the perception of reality — that is, we perceive what we can name.

It may well be that in the course of development the perceptual distinctions of the child are consolidated and structured by the signs of approval and disapproval, the shared "signs" of gesture and word which represent a major form of social reciprocity, by the symbols or standardization, coin of the realm, shared not only by parent and child, but by the community as a whole. We *accept* or *reject* (sometimes passionately) the distinctions others make, and make our own distinctions. That such control of perception by symbol may be diffuse or generalized is evident through semantics, as in Osgood's "semantic differential," which lays bare for us highly generalized systems of meaning, especially meanings which portray for us the world of action or inaction, the world of value and no value, and the world of power and no power.

We have defined the process of learning to encounter reality as a process that results in expectations, and we have defined the learning of expectations as the learning of acts of attending. Indeed, we have suggested that the world of the real might be defined in terms of attending processes. We are ready now for the question: in what sense do the attending processes structure reality?

ATTENTION, RELEVANCE, AND MEANING

In Hernández-Peón's laboratory, we see the auditory mechanism of the cat busily responding to a click, *until* a mouse is introduced into the cat's world; then, as the mouse holds attention, the physiological activity of the listening process disappears.[1] We do not now raise the question of whether the cat "suppresses" the auditory response; here, for a broad biological orientation, it shuts out the irrelevant as it pulls in the relevant. Such shutting out is a *gating* response. The movements of the mouse are *relevant*. By "relevant" is meant directly conducive to the satisfaction or frustration of needs, or at a higher level, by connection with other stimulus patterns not acting upon the organism at the time. This latter possibility would lead into Titchener's "context theory of meaning": the real has meaning. It has a context directly in terms of

[1] Geometric shapes will not function in this setting as live mice will.

needs, or in terms of patterns which are themselves ultimately related to needs.

Though we shall examine this conception critically later, it may be useful here to speak of *degrees of reality*. A smudge on a piece of paper has little meaning. Let the paper be valuable, however, as a piece of rare stock or vellum, and the smudge upon it annoys us. There is meaning. The paper is "spoiled." In another dimension, let the smudge slowly change under the light so that we see it as a child's vague tracing, an effort to draw something. If done by a little child making his first drawing, or a child with pride in his artistry, it has meaning. Or consider another possibility, that the smudge means the child was careless, thoughtless, slovenly, deserving reproach. These instances suggest that the original, undifferentiated smudge had very little meaning, but in various ways — by supplying new contexts — it became meaningful, or it became meaningful by becoming slowly more structured, turning into a sketch or a drawing. Meanings have varying degrees of articulateness and reality is dependent upon meaning.

The meanings may be very primitive. The mother holds up the sketch. The father across the room denies that it is a drawing. It does not mean anything. Closer to it, however, he may change his mind. There are degrees of relevance, degrees of meaning, and perhaps, though our usage of terms is still unclear in this matter, we shall find this useful as an approach to degrees of reality, or levels of reality.

MEANING GIVEN IN TERMS OF ACTION

However, there is another equally respected and fervently defended conception of the meaning of a stimulus impression; namely, its implications for *action*. It is not just context that gives meaning. It is a context of expected or required behavior. The meaning of "up" is first of all a motion from the earth's surface, and of "down" is a return to it. Ask a friend to define "right" and "left," "wide" and "narrow," without gesticulation; or ask him to define any abstract term without "processing" information, that is, ultimately and literally taking things from one point and putting them at another. Separating, compounding, revolving, reversing — ultimately all forms of doing — involve expansion and contraction, exclusion and inclusion. Our Latin and our Germanic roots alike trace the world of logical, numerical, and all sorts of meanings, to operations ultimately carried out by our musculature. You "see what I mean" when you "take in the idea," or you regard my ideas as "meaningless" when you cannot "sort them out." From this point of view, the real is that which has movement implications.

We can, if we like, go back to the very beginnings of the analysis (page 11) and suggest that when once you get beyond the chemical interactions of environment and world, there are always signals which say, go or come; stand or sit; ultimately sniff or turn away; move eyes towards or away, just as the objects presented are things from which we must move, or towards which we must move. The meaning of a cloud is rain, and the meaning of rain is cold and wet, and the meaning of cold and wet is retreat — while there is still time — to protection and warmth. This is *not* a statement to the effect that no other associations are aroused by clouds. There are, of course, all sorts of visual images, esthetic implications, for painter and poet, etc.

Neither is the attempt made to say that the world of meaning and the world of association are identical. We would say simply that the more the implications for action are developed, the nearer we have come to defining the meaning of a stimulus situation. This is a familiar twentieth century view comparable in subtlety and power to the context view suggested by Titchener. Our task is not to decide between them, but to suggest directions in which they may be explored, and experiments — past, present, or future — which may be relevant to the solution of the problem.

LEARNING AND ISOMORPHISM

Beyond this it might well turn out that a gradual approach towards a model which befits the real world is possible in terms of learning processes such as we have begun to sketch.

It might possibly be true that there is an isomorphism between the external structure and the inner structure of anticipations, supported as they are by inner movements, but supported also to a considerable degree by the natural or primitive self-sufficiency, goodness, structure, or order of the inner patterns insofar as they are called into action by the outer pattern. As we saw (page 19), there is some isomorphism given at a structural level, and function often has the task of enriching and developing structural potentialities (compare below, the experiments by Krech, page 48). The world of "sensory deprivation" not only lacks some of the pieces, it also lacks structural potentials. The process of conditioning can lead on into more and more conformity, based upon the primitive biological conformities and becoming ultimately dependent upon personal and social norms. In the creation of a law, there is always, as Egon Brunswik showed, a sampling from the environment; the more adequate the sample, the more adequate the personal operating law which is developed. From this viewpoint, the act of centration, based as it is upon biological realities such as figure-ground differentiation, is largely developed from early habits of attending.

FUNCTION AND STRUCTURE

So far, our concern has been basically with two kinds of processes: those which have to do with the direction, steering, or coordinating of the contact-making processes; and those which have to do with *holding* contact (page 24) with the environment. It has been presupposed that the biological structure of the individual is a primary factor, not only in specific "innate" behavior, but in the predetermination towards learning in one way rather than another, or towards learning specific things rather than other things.

Here, however, the head of an ancient enigma, important for all biology, is raised: can function change structure? Ordinarily the structure of a machine, and for that matter the structure of an egg or of a nerve cell or of a human brain, is conceived to limit function, to set function, to establish priority of one function over another, and in Sherrington's phrase, to provide the "integrative action." Part of the psychiatrist's and psychologist's sharp distinction between "organic" conditions, on the one hand and "functional," on the other, is based upon the assumption that functional activity does not materially alter structure. Even a physical illness, like some cases of arthritis which appear to arise from psychological conflict, is often held to be "reversible." However, there is often a hesitating admission that a certain number of such effects are irreversible, that is, that function has resulted, over time, in a biochemical "lesion," a minute, anatomically identifiable or even a large and more visible lesion that the microscope can detect.

Actually, upon close confrontation of the problem, a great deal of evidence has been obtained not only in psychosomatic medicine with its reference to chronic damage as a result of functional anomalies and stresses, but even in everyday normal life in which growth in one direction rather than another has been seen to be a matter of the biochemical consequences of one persisting function rather than another. Especially dramatic is the line of evidence which has begun to accumulate since the work of Donald Hebb. On the one hand, his conception of the "cell assembly" postulated that functional changes could effect the material organization of the brain, and much subsequent work on sensory deprivation has supported such a view. The experiments, for example, of Krech and his collaborators at the University of California at Berkeley have apparently shown, with adequate replication, that an *enriched* environment for baby rodents results in measurably thicker brain cortex, and also in relatively greater concentrations of acetylcholine; that these animals from *average* environments are again notably more developed both in terms of brain anatomy and in terms of brain chemistry than those reared in an *impoverished* environment. When one thinks of the stupidity and the declining I.Q.'s of institutionalized children who sit by the hour with nothing to do, one begins to set up bold hypotheses to define the relation of brain structure to the functional realities which work upon it. There seems to be a considerable promise that we shall soon understand structure in biochemical terms much more fully by having seen that the *use* of nerve cells in particular ways can in fact change them.

It is indeed likely also that the many biochemical studies of schizophrenia will begin to close in on the gap between the "organic" and the "functional" interpretations, especially so if genetic factors are conceived in terms of their biochemical interaction with environmental factors of use, which in the case of the socially neglected, impoverished, and frightened, may limit the capacity for social adaptation. Some studies seem to show that constitutional instability of the autonomic system predisposes towards biochemical irregularities and instabilities from which damage to the central nervous system can, in time, flow. Exactly this type of biochemical damage to the nerve cell growth is well known in the case of phenylpyruvics, those whose genetic constitutions include a gene predisposing the "errors of metabolism," in which phenylpyruvic acid appears in the urine. But "fate" is relative and the right diet can partly correct for such "errors."

Another line of inquiry along the lines originally suggested by Hebb is the investigation of sheer differentiation in central nervous tissue as a result of exercise. It occurred to Wiesel and Hubel to rear kittens with the lids of one eye sutured together. Later, with microphotography, it was shown that marked histological changes in the visual pathways fed by the deprived eye had occurred. Thus when there was light in one half of the visual field of the kitten, while there was none in the other, post-mortem studies showed a very striking difference in the growth on the two sides.

From the present viewpoint these are all cases in which the function *does* change structure; moreover, the fine structure of the outer environment is conveyed inward to play a part in establishing the fine structure of the inner world. For us the outer structure has become real; first, because we have to act in these terms; later, because the inner holds the mirror up to nature; the inner has become one with the outer. It is movement towards isomorphism.

6

The Reality of the
World Within

So far, our concern has been with the response of the individual living system to the structure of the external environment. This is exactly half of the total world with which we are concerned. Eddington notes that the human body is, in a sense, geometrically halfway between the smallest and the largest things of which we have knowledge; namely, the electron and the universe. However this may be, man is, in a sense, the measure of all things; at least, from his own point of view, a geometric mean between the infinitely little and the infinitely big.

We can no longer, in these days of biology, medicine, and Claude Bernard's "inner environment," write as if reality were simply a knowable thing or process *outside us*. On the contrary, the knowing process reaches in, and in following the Greek maxim, "know thyself," it finds that there is just as much complexity, just as much that eludes us, yet calls for scrutiny, as there is at the astronomical level. The reflector telescope is a powerful engine, and so is the electron microscope. That is what is meant by saying that exactly half the problem of the real lies within.

Here Bleuler with his magnificent introduction to the world of self-deception, the world he called "de-realist," somehow missed the boat. For him, the process of "autism" is the process by which a real outer world is distorted — "de-realized" by inner dynamics. But we likewise distort our view of the *inner* world; indeed, the inner world is both the "distorter" and the "distorted." And to add another paradox, the inner world with its craving for reality (page 109), may insist on sweeping away the illusions begotten by our defective sense processes. There is no eternal alliance between the "inner" and the "unreal." The problem of learning to perceive, to understand, and to use the *inner real* is as fundamental as the problem of coping with the *outer real*. Cognitive confusion is a failure of the knowing process, and it fails just as much through defect in grasping what is within, as through defect in grasping what is without. Indeed, the knowing process stands, so to speak, on the bridge.

Ego on the Bridge Between Inner and Outer

This ambiguity is reflected in the two connotations of the term "subjective." (1) The word is used to describe the escapist fumblings and gropings of a man lacking the refinements of the mathematical, logical, and scientific skills which order sense impressions and abstract from them. (2) The term is also used to define the real inner order of our human life, which needs to be observed and studied — shall we say — "objectively"? We become aware that the *subject* can be the *object* of our inquiry, and that we may be lost in "subjectivism" when observing *either* the outer *or* the inner. From the viewpoint of the best observation and reasoning at our command, our job, using all the resources we can find, is to look at the world within us with the same sharp scientific scrutiny we use in looking at the world without. In other words, reality is not simply that which belongs to the exteroceptive field; it belongs just as much to the interoceptive.

The thoughtful critic may well reply that from the very beginning the world within is a world of *disorder*, and the world without a world of *order*, as known by science. But surely, the world within is being rapidly sorted out with all the remarkable techniques of modern genetics, embryology, physiology, biochemistry, and "input" from inner vegetative and muscular sources. Surely it has been found that the world without owes its orderliness in considerable degree to the imposition upon it of those structured thinking principles which have arisen just as much from the inner necessities as from the outer pressures.

Similarly, the question may be raised: if both "outer" and "inner" are subject to systematic and objective scrutiny, where is the "knowing" consciousness located and what are the conditions under which objectivity about both worlds of information may be achieved? In partial answer, we may rely upon David Rapaport's formulation of the issue. The ego — the organized expression of human individuality — utilizes the instinctual energies, but at the same time guides the executive functions which make possible both the mastery of impulse within and of behavior. It can achieve autonomy only if the turbulent surge of the world within can be kept at bay, while at the same time the crushing weight of external stimulation can be kept from exercising overwhelming control. It can succeed only if the capacity for firm testing of reality — sifting, sorting, and controlling its energies, development of buffer systems equal to the stress — can be built up through the long socialization process. There is a tiny node of security, and even of power, for the ego, if it can maintain a measure of control over both the relentless systems which strive to impose their massive force upon it.

It is a delicate balance that the ego maintains. Harold Voth, in contemplating the modern typologies which have classified personalities in terms of their closeness to the outer environment or their tendency to fall back upon the inner environment, has developed the concepts "ego distant" and "ego close" to represent respectively those who withdraw into an inner safety and those who welcome the challenging em-

braces of the outer world. He has shown, by systematic clinical interviewing, by means of the Rorschach test, and especially by means of the autokinetic test (the apparent movement
of a tiny point of light which is in fact stationary in the dark
room) that subjects can be arranged in a series from extremely "ego close" to extremely "ego distant"; that, in fact,
most reasonably well-adjusted people are, as required by Rapaport's thesis, somewhere in the middle. They are people who,
when they look upon the stationary light, "allow" it to move
a little, keep it under some sort of surveillance, do not allow
it to writhe and glide too extravagantly far from the sober
actuality that it is not moving at all!

Is the "Inner" Not Real?

Lest the reader think we are not quite serious in our sober
declaration that the inner is every bit as "real" as the outer,
let us deal for a moment with the view that human beings
"really see" and "really hear" and "really touch" the outer
world, whereas they only "remember," or "imagine" when they
have no exteroceptive contacts. Looked at more closely, this
seems to mean that humans, and indeed their pets and beasts
of burden and the world of animal life with which they have
actual communication, share an exteroceptive world. It is a
relatively objective, firm, and even changeable world where
you can point out and share with me, and with your dog,
things immediately real to you. At the same time it means that
the things you share at a visceral level, so to speak — the
things you share in terms of a common past with neighborhood or family members, the sifted essence of the meanings
of life, the things that most people regard as "real," and the
things specifically related to the personal realities of one's
own individual life history — have to be anchored on the
within. The process by which a little encapsulated speck of
living matter was able to maintain its integrity from the buffets
of sea and land was largely dependent upon inner messages;
and it has continued and expanded until the maintenance of
this kind of inner structure is a priceless part of our human

treasure. It will not serve humans very well if they fall into the habit of regarding the events within as in some sense "less real" than the events without.

In American life it has been rather bad form to uphold too vigorously the reality of the world within, for two very simple reasons: (1) the strenuous tasks of a geographically expanding and industrially growing society make external contacts more reputable than internal; (2) instruments devised to make observation more accurate — the extended eye of the microscope, the extended ear of the electronic pickup, the resonator, the hearing aid — have given us more precision, up to the present moment, than the sensory processes within us have so far discovered alone.

Perhaps this is because we *wish it to be so.* Perhaps by means of the mechanisms of turning away, undoing, denial, and the other well-established dynamic principles by which we refuse close attention, and especially close analysis, we turn from that which threatens the integrity of our egos, including this world of inner experience. It may indeed be, by virtue of the very principles just quoted above from David Rapaport, that we stand on guard not only against the massive force of the inner world, but against getting acquainted with its inhabitants, its component parts. Perhaps we would feel overwhelmed if we knew the inhabitants too closely. Perhaps the process of placing a taboo, especially upon the broad gamut of the experiences Freud calls libidinal, would make differentiation a sin or a crime, or at least an expression of bad taste. Perhaps condemnation is added to initial clumsiness and to the negative reinforcements or punishments which have come when one sees that which is socially disreputable, or at least personally repugnant to parents. There is surely more to it than this; perhaps all these factors, and more too, are involved in the unrealism of our habitual denial of reality to the very real *real* of the inner world.

Certainly related to all these mechanisms, by which we keep ourselves from sharp perception of the inner world of the real, stands the process which Else Frenkel-Brunswik called "tolerance and intolerance of ambiguity." To some of us an illusion or even a mild hallucination is intriguing, or a bit challenging. To others, because the thing is both real and unreal, it is ambiguous, and because ambiguous, intolerable. Some may see the horseman shown in a pattern of lights in the psychology laboratory as he jumps from one point to another when the requisite electrical switches are thrown on or off. To others, because it is well known that this horseman is "really" sitting there in the etched outline of the figure, and it is certain that he can *not* be jumping, the experience is disagreeable indeed. If a careful count is made, the horseman spends a good deal less time in the air for such an observer than for the observer who has less intolerance of ambiguity. The concept of intolerance of ambiguity is a convenient one in the classification of persons for whom the real is the objective external order with "no nonsense about it," while the kind of flexibility described here under the term "intolerance of ambiguity" is convenient in reference to the habit of assigning a pretty large number of our experiences to the doubtful region of a sort of second-class reality.

How the "Inner" Is Perceived

But there is another reason for failure to evaluate and even to observe the world within. This lies in the nature of the thresholds of perception. A universal habit of psychologists is to define thresholds in terms of the amounts of stimulation, specifically, the amounts of energy, required to set a sensory process going. The "all-or-none law" often means in practice that the impact of a given energy upon a receptor fails to achieve a value permitting the wave of sensory excitation to pass along the afferent fiber towards the brain; whereas a bit more energy would have done the trick, triggering the nerve fiber, getting the message through to the second nerve cell in the relay, perhaps the third, and perhaps the fourth. Different receptors have different thresholds — the thresholds for pain, for example, are very low — and the threshold varies from one part of the body to another. Note, for instance, how fine the differentiation of two points may be at the tip of the tongue, and how poor it may be in the small of the back. Now, the thresholds are rather high in the inner sensory life of man, at least for the warmth, cold, and pressure detected in the interior, and for those diffuse experiences associated with hunger, thirst, oxygen need, sex need, and fatigue, malaise, and the stimuli associated with "mood." The affective states are much like these inner sensations in some ways. They are "massive" rather than "precise"; they are like the "protopathic" rather than the "epicritic" experiences found when a severed nerve in the arm makes possible a differentiation of sensations. The experiences of disgust, delight, surprise, or amusement seem like varieties of sensations, and the sexual has often been called "sensuous" on the grounds that sensory values make up a large part of the experience.

However, it is worth noting in this connection that recent studies by Russian physiologists, such as Bykov and his associates, have emphasized numerous "interoceptors" in the visceral organs of animals and man. Such interoceptors differ anatomically and respond selectively to differing types of stimulation. In an early attempt at demonstrating interoceptive two-point discrimination, Makarov found that human subjects could differentiate rapid, successive electrical stimulation of gastric mucosa 8 cm. apart. It should be clear, therefore, that an anatomical and physiological basis for fairly fine discrimination of interoceptive sensation exists. It may well be that our high threshold levels for such sensation and its differentiation are in part functional, or even voluntary, for reasons suggested above.

A great deal of the inner sensory world varies moment by moment and hour by hour at a point well below thresholds for good description, so that our moods vary. Even moods which last so long that we call them "temperament" are like inner sensations but crude, coarse, hard to observe, and certainly hard to evaluate. When we try to report on what we mean by a cheerful temperament, or what we mean if we say that this morning we are cheerful but by afternoon we will be glum again, we seem to be dealing with complex *interpretations* rather than with descriptions of sensory data. We may, in fact, have a great deal of massive, subthreshold excitation going on all the time. Relatively little of it takes sensory form even when the trained observer tries to find evidence of specific "organic" sensations. A person may act as if he were thirsty, or a habitual smoker may act in an obvious way with reference to his tobacco need, without having been conscious of the need state. Clark Hull's pipe-smokers, after experiencing smoking "satisfaction" from sham pipes which they thought were filled, "lit up" as they left the laboratory. A person may, even without benefit of repression, respond to massive visceral tension — appetitive or aversive — while not knowing at all (at the conscious level) that this is so.

INTEROCEPTIVE STIMULATION AND THE "SENSE OF REALITY"

Now there is a very special reason for considering here these rich and varied types of subthreshold inner excitation, for the "sense of reality" is to a large degree determined by the elaboration of this kind of sensory experience. From Pierre Janet and his "memories which are too real" to the modern psychoanalytically-oriented psychiatrist's concern with "un-reality feelings" as related to "depersonalization," there is evidence that awareness of the real is itself partly an expression of the subthreshold condition in the interior of the trunk, especially the cardiovascular and gastrointestinal systems. A swimming head or a growling stomach may mean that "nothing is real today." At another extreme, the experience of highly vivid or incandescent reality, associated with some types of religious or esthetic mysticism and with some modern drug investigations, may accentuate the sharpness of definition to a point where both the inner and the outer cosmos of reality reach by a wide margin their highest intensity, their sharpest definition, as the "very real," just because the exteroceptive definition of the world is controlled and submerged by the messages from within.

A medical friend, experimenting with drugs which enabled the red blood cells to carry far more oxygen than usual, came dramatically to the expression "ferric consciousness" (pertaining to iron), by which he intended to convey that the sharpness, the intensity, the meaning of reality was no longer dependent upon sheer neurophysiological function, but was expressly the product of the *iron* of the red blood cells capable of carrying this overload of oxygen. For him, from the flattest to the sharpest affective level in daily life is but a hand's breadth compared to the *ocean-like* distance between nonferric and ferric consciousness. This fancy, or whimsy, shows the need of the ecstatic experiencer of the expanding real to take hold of a chemical symbol to show how far his psychological state differs from those known to most men.

But whereas the reality described above depends partly upon inner processes, it is usually not directly experienced as inner process. Rather, it tends to be oriented to an outer cosmos. When one looks more closely, one begins to doubt whether these experiences of supernal reality could be as intense if the experiencer were at the time looking at his interoceptive activities. He would, at any rate, have to learn to observe them by lowering their thresholds, and by developing a progressive conceptual differentiation, like a tea taster, or a wine sampler, learning to pick out faint elements of "aroma" or "bouquet," which are beyond the capacity of the novice. It is possible that this type of analytical and perceptual training would actually weaken or destroy the perceptual wholes, or at any rate, their meaning. Here again, it is too early to be sure. We have not trained the experiencer to describe this kind of experience as the tea taster and wine sampler are trained. It is safer to say that the exteroceptive world is the world each of us *recognizes,* the world we differentiate, look at, and compare piece by piece and phase by phase, while the interoceptive world is generally massive, relatively undifferentiated, and relatively unchallenging to the perspective eye of curiosity. The exteroceptive is easy to *share,* the interoceptive hard to share.

INTERNAL SCANNING

But whether we avow the fact or not, experimental evidence has been coming in recently to indicate that many of us carry out a continuous process of internal scanning, exactly as we carry out the process of external scanning. The most obvious case is the child's — or adults — watching his own dream, a process which was recognized by the brilliant insight of Kleitman as he observed rapid horizontal eye movements behind the eyelids of sleeping subjects. We know today that dreams are scanned just as outer worlds are scanned, and that memory materials are scanned by horizontal eye movement, very much as the hallucinatory materials of dreams are scanned. We know that the power and the delicacy of visual seeking and scanning movements are employed with regard to those maps and designs for living which some of us utilize in planning the day or the life well in advance. We know that failure to relax and to go to sleep is often expressed in the inability or unwillingness to give up the eager, nervous eye movements directed towards the precious things of the imagination which we cannot give up or even allow to go to their rest.

There may be a paradox here. We are beginning to concern ourselves with internal scanning, but we are *still* describing exteroceptive organs. We look within; we look at dreams and memories. But when we want more evidence than sight can afford, we listen, as did Socrates, to an inner voice. We bring back the voice of father and mother. Or indeed, when we become frightened or anxious, we may, in auditory hallucinations, make real to ourselves the threats or accusations which once came from without and now come from within us. Somehow, then, though we are talking about an inner world, it is the machinery of exteroception that is involved.

But this statement still misses a fundamental point. It is not literally the eyes or the ears that bespeak the scanning process. It is the act of attending. *Look* at some bright object in the room, but attend to something quite different. You will find — and many a laboratory investigator has confirmed and made more specific what you can observe in the first ten seconds of your own experiment — that to attend is a more complex process (compare page 24) than to look or to listen. It makes use of the peripheral machinery in the organs of sense, but the central process is to attend, as James has pointed out, by *drawing objects into the center of clearest awareness*. This is what you do with interoceptive material, whether you are looking or not. You have some vague internal distress. It may be difficult to tell what it is, or even where it is. But the internist who has to decide whether there is something seriously wrong or not, may have to press, both in a literal and in a metaphorical sense, to find out what it is; and the night after you see him, as you review the experience, you may find yourself in your internal scanning, doing relatively little with your eyes or ears, and a great deal with the attending processes. Through them you bring back the pressure, strain, warm, cold, or pain experiences which you described as well as you could to the doctor. You recapitulate such sensations, mark off, sunder one from another, emphasize, regroup, reinterpret, making sense as well as you can out of this material by a rich internal scanning, focusing, and reporting process.

There is then a process of internal scanning, and it is not limited solely to the use of exteroceptors turned inwards. We do, however, emphasize that exteroceptive modes turned inwards play an important part; indeed, the main reality to be stressed here is the fact of internal scanning, and not the agencies by which this is effected.

INDIVIDUAL DIFFERENCES IN INTERNAL SCANNING

Likewise important is the matter of profound individual differences in the disposition to internal scanning, as compared with external. It has become possible, by experiment and administration of self-report schedules, to get evidence that one person deploys his energies largely with reference to his inner world, and another largely with regard to the outer world. The one retreats from and the other advances towards the field of exteroceptive stimulation. This is related to Jung's extraversion-introversion, but has become somewhat more sharply defined. As we saw above (page 52), Harold Voth has called such individuals respectively "ego close" and "ego distant." While there is probably a more or less normal bell-shaped curve from one extreme to the other, there are enough extreme cases to offer handles for a variety of important psychiatric problems. For example, the therapy to be undertaken with a person making outer-reality contacts with great difficulty may depend upon the kind of handles, the kind of emotional investments he has in the outer, as contrasted with the inner world, as well as upon the stability or rigidity with which he maintains a given position on this continuum. An assumption of relatively stable individual positions on this continuum would imply that what feeds into a person from the rich outer world makes even richer what is already awaiting such stimulation, but that a person already preoccupied with the riches of the inner world will bar out the external, which is too close, and will make for himself a snugger nest of internal realities.

Our own interest here in habits of scanning leads us to a somewhat different answer to the question as to the necessary consistency or generality of these general personal tendencies to be ego-close or ego-distant. Voth would believe, for example, that a great deal of practice in external scanning might make one increase one's investment in the outer world. Our own position would be different, partly because we agree with Rapaport's conception that there must be some sort of balance between the outer and the inner. We believe that there is only one scanning process, whether it be directed to outer or to inner things. And from this it would follow, regardless of whether an individual is predominantly disposed to attend to inner or outer realities, that practice in *external scanning*, and the refinement which follows upon it, might well strengthen his capacity for refined internal perception.

Inner Stimulation and Feedback

Under the impact of science and engineering, and the biological analysis of impulses which took on new character as each sensory-motor adjustment was made, the concept of *feedback* has begun to crowd into the center of scientific awareness. Norbert Wiener's brilliant coining of the term "cybernetics" sharpened the universal rationale — supported by mathematical analysis — of the phenomenon by which the "servo-mechanisms" of industry are brought into relation to the cycles of self-excitation, and of environment-organism interaction, upon which such principles as homeostatic balance are based.

The feedback studies of today in the behavioral sciences are experimentally precise, well structured for space and time, and as in the work of Wiener, mathematically sophisticated. A convenient illustration is the study of visual feedback in eye-hand coordination in the studies by K. U. Smith and W. M. Smith, by which temporal variations in the supply of visual information during a manual task make the difference between effective and clumsy work; or the studies of delayed auditory feedback, by which a speaker can almost instantly be demoralized by feeding into his ears an off-timed report on his own utterances.

It has been well shown by contemporary Soviet investigators that proprioceptive and interoceptive stimuli may function within a classical conditioning model essentially as exteroceptive stimuli function. Proprioceptive and interoceptive stimuli guide the organism in its continuous locomotor activity, and as this becomes more consistently "operant," goal-directed, or "purposive," in other words, insofar as features of a situation condition the same locomotor manipulative and other operant responses, the proprioceptive and interoceptive components take on a steering function.

At a more complex clinical level, Holzman has shown that the tape-recorded voice of a young adult describing the first job he ever held can make him suddenly and disturbingly aware of his voice, especially of various idiosyncrasies which he cannot bear to recognize. Then follows a complicated series of *tours de force* by which he comes to reject his voice, and then comes to terms with it.

Closely related to such delayed or disturbed or disturbing feedback which throw slightly off-center the ordinary, every-day, accepted feedbacks upon which our lives are based, there is the process of central control of sensory functions by which we accept, reject, and filter the evidence of what we are doing. We do it, and at the same time, make ready the defense against recognizing it. We fan the flame with one hand and try to put the fire out with the other. (More will be said of this when we turn to the issue of inhibition in Chapter 9.)

PROPRIOCEPTIVE "NOISE" AS DEFENSE

We make effective reality contact partly by adjusting the movements of eyes, head, trunk, etc., so that the sensory surfaces can get what they need to carry out a plan which is in the course of execution, partly also, of course, by making ready the surfaces which will be needed a moment later. Our bodily tension system as a whole may be aimed specifically against threats and at preparing the acts of rejection and parrying which may be needed. But it is sometimes diffusely or totalistically oriented towards a sort of rigid rejection of all reality, a sort of massive elevation of thresholds and rejection of information. We would expect transfer from one kind of defensive operation to another, on the basis of the ordinary principles of practice. So we would expect, let us say, that skill in cutting out social contact with a father or mother, will lead — if it defends against stress and pain — to rejection of messages from siblings, from playmates, from teachers, and ultimately, from the world as a whole. There may be such a thing as a generalized gating out, the proprioceptive system acting as the gater. We tighten the body; we drum with the fingers; tap with the feet; gasp, over-breathe, and constantly invent new devices for introducing internal "noise" by which to deafen us to unpleasant messages; we chomp and make busy counterstimulation which will have a distraction value. At the same time, we may need to avert our eyes; whether the lids are open or not is secondary in importance. We may learn to look away in the specific focused sense of ocular behavior or in the broader sense of transferred and generalized aversive responses.

The Norwegian psychiatrist, Braatoy, found that patients with chronic "arm neurosis" (forearms tight and rigid to the point of interference with their manual activity) could be led, through verbal interchanges and effective massage, to a relaxation in the forearm muscles. Upon such treatment there would suddenly supervene a "flood of painful memories." As we would expect in terms of Wilhelm Reich's conception of "character armor," the muscular system had been rendered sufficiently tight to inhibit inner impulses, especially impulses related to aggression against the father and fraught with conflictual and painful components. With the effective defense in terms of arm neurosis — which prevented the execution of combative movements in harmony with combative fantasies — it was possible for the patient to set the whole perceptual machinery into rigid patterns and freeze the whole psychological situation; that is, until the therapist let the cat out of the bag; then the muscles could no longer keep the flood of painful memories in check. The defensive operations are partly *general,* in the form of raising the *general* level of self-distraction of muscular work, but partly *specific,* in the form of blocking aggressive components in the arms.

PROPRIOCEPTIVE FEEDBACK AND INNER CONTROL

Braatoy's work dates from the late 1940's and the beginning of the 1950's. At that time there were available, through the labors of Jacobson, Max, and others, techniques using fairly good electronic devices, which made it possible to throw upon a screen the visual record of striped muscle activity, which both the experimenter and the subject himself could see. This kind of visual feedback from proprioceptive activity offered such obvious promise that there was pressure towards greater and greater refinement in instrumentation. Thus Hefferline trained his subjects to open their mouths so gradually, so delicately, that they could, so to speak, write upon an electronic screen the intensity of the jaw muscle contractions. The experimenter sat on one side, the subject on the other side of a gauge upon which the electronic display indicated just how wide open the mouth was. By paying attention to the input (proprioceptive information from the jaw converted into visual form), while observing the electronic record, the subject could develop a certain respect and confidence in his own capacity to evaluate the tensing of the jaw muscle. And with good reason; it was found that when the visual information was cut off, the subject could rather precisely determine, by proprioception alone, how well he was doing.

From this kind of experiment Davidowitz, in Hefferline's laboratory, went on to a study of specific finger movements which, if carefully executed, give each time just about the same electronic record; that is, after a training period, the subject obtains voluntary control not over gross muscular pattern alone, but over quite precise variations of the activity of a single muscle. This begins to offer substantial hope that even without exteroceptive information, one may begin to control the inner world as one controls the outer world through visual feedback. This goal is, of course, like the goals of the ancient yoga system, and it is not surprising to find today, on the part of both Western and Indian scholars, a hope for future East-West exchange of ideas regarding self-control of this type.

So far proprioceptive feedback has interested us. Soviet investigators have gone somewhat further than those of the West in applying these same concepts to the *interoceptive* world. In the Soviet Union there has been interest in gaining control not only of striped musculature (which after all we do, of course, regard as "voluntary musculature"), but over unstriped musculature as well. It appears that Lisina has been successful in training subjects to regulate the cardiovascular system, as for example, in the rate and force of the heartbeat, by working out a rational step-by-step basis of such control. This has enabled the subject to carry out internal scanning to the point of successful identification of certain bodily changes which go with various types of control of the pulse, and through the inward arousal of images and words appropriate to such action of the heart, to control the heart with a regularity not previously reported in accredited publications. Unfortunately some doubt continues to surround the success of Lisina's training methods. But even so, there is recent, unambiguous evidence from American laboratories demonstrating "voluntary" control over heart rate variability (Hnatiow & Lang) and heart rate itself (Brener & Hothersall) using exteroceptive feedback, indicating the possibility of "voluntary" control of unstriped musculature.

Lisina's results, if replicated and fully understood, would mean that we are on the threshold of a vast new world of internal control both at the perceptual level and at the level of voluntary control. It is hard to see how the world of the real could be rigidly limited to the external environment if control should reach this level. This still would lack direct control of sensation, image, and feeling; but through the control of motor components, both striped and unstriped muscles, and even through the partial control of endocrine organs and inhibiting processes exercised by the central nervous system downwards upon some of its afferent parts (compare page 85), we might look towards a greatly extended world of organized and insightful self-control. It would be a self-control based upon perceptual clarity and order and of course, upon that autonomous exercise of ego function to which we referred in the discussion above (compare Rapaport, page 52). Another important chapter is being written by Joe Kamiya, in whose studies the subject, through feedback, learns to control his own alpha rhythm and goes on to the voluntary control of other brain waves, as their subjective counterparts are examined.

SUMMARY

This chapter has ranged so widely over largely uncharted territory that the reader may welcome a reprise before going on even further in the next chapter. In what has preceded we have emphatically placed the inner world, the "subjective" mass of internal sensations, upon the same reality footing as the world without and have insisted that order in this inner world can become known through the methods of science. The traditional reluctance to do so seems to us to be based upon a culture bound bias to regard *only* the products of exteroception as "objective" and therefore real, a bias, abetted perhaps by the apparently high threshold for awareness of internal stimulation and the more diffuse, undifferentiated character of sensations arising from it.

We have suggested that while much of internal stimulation may be below the threshold of awareness, it nonetheless affects the sense of what is "real" and "unreal," moods and affects. We have suggested that there is a continuous process of "internal scanning" depending in part upon exteroceptors turned inward and characterized by acts of *attending* to inner events.

Feedback from proprioceptors plays an important role in coordinating and steering motoric behavior, and may also serve a defensive function in the form of internal "noise" that masks painful, unacceptable ideas. That control over very fine muscle movements has been achieved experimentally, through training in attention to proprioception alone, hints at the possibility of voluntary control even over unstriped muscle effectors and thus internal organs through the use of interoceptive information.

7

Inner Controls

Since we have held that the feeling life is in many respects comparable to the sensory life, we must ask whether the principle of feedback does not apply as well to interoceptive as to proprioceptive input. There is more obvious proprioceptive input from the sensory adjustments, of course: the movement of eyes, head, trunk, and limbs in the process of responding and the anticipation of fresh encounters with the environment. From the very nature of the case we should not expect as much active movement in the service of contact with the world within. Thus, the exteroceptive system is intimately dependent for its effective work upon proprioceptive assistance, while it appears that the interoceptive system is not.

Another reason why science has, in recent decades, tied the proprioceptive system conceptually to the exteroceptive is that we encounter much more of the "voluntary" when proprioception is involved; in fact, the large striped muscles are often properly called the voluntary muscles, and each of us has developed voluntary control of the body and of its contact with the environment largely through the combined utilization of proprioceptive and exteroceptive systems (compare above, page 62). Human beings do not ordinarily learn voluntary control of the organ responses from which interoception flows, such as the gastrointestinal and cardiovascular responses. At times, the question has arisen as to whether the unstriped musculature of the gastrointestinal and the unique muscle tissue of the cardiovascular systems can ever become truly subject to voluntary control. These doubts express the general inclination of Western science to the view that in some deep sense the exteroceptive system is a system for "encountering reality," while there is thought to be a fatal subjectivism, a sort of "withinness" about the interoceptive system. From this viewpoint, the only way we can change our emotional and other affective responses is by changing the outward situation upon which these feeling responses depend.

Actually, this is one of the many paradoxes in the Western conception of the subject-object relation, for the cardinal principal of ethics is usually held to lie in self-control, and he who ruleth his spirit is greater than he that taketh the city. The pinnacle of ethical rightness in the highest expression of Western thought lies not merely in doing right, but in feeling right in the ultimate sense of an absolute ethic. There is the assumption that man has voluntary control of his feeling life, as well as of his action life. "Grace" is an exception, but grace is from God, not from man. One of the many charges against psychoanalysis, in moral terms, has been directed against its emphasis upon man's helplessness in controlling his affective life. The effort to control hostility, for example, is seen in the form of blind redirection of our hostility to others, who are perhaps innocent parties. The kindness and generosity we would cultivate is conceived to be reaction formation against cruelty.

Voluntary Control of Autonomic Functions

Clearly the factual issues here are of grave importance both for a theory of man, and for everyday morals. The issue can be phrased in terms of a series of questions about feedback from the interoceptive system, notably from all the organs innervated by the autonomic nervous system, and if our conception of the development of voluntary control is correct, ultimately the voluntary control of autonomic functions as well. We briefly review evidences and opinions current in this field.

While Pavlov worked on the conditioning of vegetative responses, notably those of the digestive system, Bekhterev in the same era studied conditioned avoidance responses carried out by the striped musculature of arm and hand. It is characteristic of the modern era of doubts that today some doubt whether Pavlov's was true autonomic conditioning, others whether there is any type of Pavlovian conditioning, in the strict sense, *except* the autonomic. (We refer those who have lingering doubts about the possibility of true autonomic conditioning to Malmo's careful 1965 study. In these experiments he demonstrated heart rate conditioning to a tone, unambiguously free of any skeletal muscle or sensitization mediation.) We have presented (page 40) examples of both vegetative-autonomic and striped muscle-cerebrospinal conditioning, and can justify this position at least in the sense of referring to numerous studies which show that the principles, the broad generalizations derived from the study of the one system, apply also to the study of the other system. If such generalizations are valid — and apparently the evidence is now positive — the connections between the exteroceptive cortical projection centers and the pleasure centers are not essentially different from the connections between centers for proprioceptive and interoceptive functions and the pleasure centers. It appears probable that the conditions for the development of more complex learning (higher-order conditioning, second-signal system, etc.) are similar in the two systems. Insofar as the execution of a conditioned response of any sort changes the outer environment, there will be exteroceptive feedback. Moreover, if there is a steady stream of input from both proprioceptive and interoceptive systems, these would inevitably converge, flow in upon the cortical centers, and upon the pleasure centers involved in the current action. It would therefore follow that there would have to be more or less simultaneous concurrent proprioceptive and interoceptive feedback as voluntary action is being learned, and after its acquisition, while it is being smoothly carried out. Interoceptive probably functions like proprioceptive feedback.

Now as far as the critical evidence is concerned, there have been a number of efforts, notably such as those quoted by Wenger and his collaborators to show that adepts in the yoga system of India acquire such unusual inner control as to arrest the heartbeat, or that other extraordinary physiological inhibitions and exaggerations have occurred. With the instrumentation used, it became clear that in many cases the heart had not actually stopped, but the force of the beat had diminished to the point where it was well below the subjective threshold, though the electrocardiogram still showed it beating. The testimony of the adept must therefore be taken with a grain of salt. The question has been raised whether any of the unusual types of voluntary control of autonomic functions are properly authenticated. But in turn, a question arises as to the sensitivity of the equipment. There is at least the suggestion in the as-yet-unreplicated work of Lisina (page 65) that the subject can be trained to detect faint interoceptive input, and after recognizing it well, can learn to assume voluntary control of its arousal, and in turn, voluntary utilization of these central representations to produce cardiovascular changes of exactly the sort now in question.

It would appear likely, all things considered, that autonomic turbulence probably provides feedback much as the cerebrospinal axis does. We have already noted (page 56) that the input from interoceptive systems may be intrinsically (that is, anatomically) less differentiated than that which comes from the proprioceptive system, and that experimental work so far suggests severe limitation in the training of the observer in noting the quantitative and qualitative variations in his own internal messages. However, these issues have never been carefully explored, and it is quite possible that sheer differences in the kind of experience in the opening weeks and months of life — in which the adult world is constantly varying and enriching the exteroceptive and proprioceptive possibilities and doing almost nothing at all to enrich the interoceptive — may be of major weight. The importance of learning to know one-self at the inside level is so great that the issue must be contested from every angle until the evidence is clear.

Of course, if there is less specificity of input or poorer dif-ferentiation in capacity for interoceptive messages, it would follow that there is probably less trainability, less opportunity for transfer from one class of interoceptive experience to other classes of interoceptive input, and also from interoceptive to exteroceptive and proprioceptive input. But the question of trainability is somewhat distinct from that of sheer differenti-ating capacity prior to training, and it is even possible that basic trainability in and capacity for transfer are somewhat different things.

"INPUT" FROM THE BRAIN

We have been describing input from receptors, and have said almost nothing at all about the types of input which have recently yielded to experimental study through *direct stimu-lation of the brain,* especially in the conscious subject under local anesthesia. Penfield and his collaborators, operating on patients subject to convulsive disorders, have brought back specific memories over and over again from the excitation of the same spot in the cerebral cortex. Most of the studies have to do with patients in whom excision of brain tissue has been determined because of their proneness to convulsions. In gen-eral, however, the course of the experimentation seems to run smoothly, with no evidence of any abnormal state in the pa-tient at the time of the electrical excitation. In Penfield's studies, upon exposure of the temporal lobe cortex to a specific stimulus, one gets the sudden arousal of memories, as for ex-ample the following:

> J.T. was startled when, as the result of temporal stimulation, he heard, as he lay in the operating room, the voices of his "cousins Bessie and Ann Wheliow," so that he cried out, "Yes, Doctor, yes, Doctor. Now I hear people laughing — my friends, in South Africa." It was obvious that this experience

seemed to him different from an ordinary recollection. It forced itself upon his attention suddenly and unexpectedly.

When he reconsidered the matter a fortnight later, he said it had seemed to him that he was with his cousins and that they were all laughing together at something, although he could not say what the subject of their merriment might be. The recollection, as far as it went, was vivid and detailed.

Although the description may suggest a hallucinatory state, such scenes are experienced by the subject as vivid memories, more vivid than he could arouse by his own effort. Yet such memories are in no way capable of confusion with the actual "here and now" reality of the operating room, the table on which he lies, or the situation of the experiment involving the conversation with the surgeon. This seems to be a remarkable instance of direct contact with the past as mediated by memory, which would ordinarily require the roundabout means of a verbal inquiry; it would thus be similar to the direct excitation of affect through the pleasure centers, as contrasted with the more roundabout way of exciting affect by stimulating the skin or the viscera (page 21).

But the concept of making contact with time in an unusual way comprises a deeper and more complex reality, which Penfield and his collaborators have sketched out; namely, the fact that there is a general proneness to time disorientation in persons subject to temporal lobe-type convulsion. The person in whom these memories were elicited by excitation of Regions 15 and 16 was also subject to the experience of "having been there before," known to psychiatry as *déjà vu*. There is much to suggest that the temporal lobe is, in a certain sense, a specialized center for orientation to time, space, and person, and orientation in time has been studied in a variety of ways through the examination of lesions in many patients and through post-mortem examinations of those whose brains did not function properly in time orientation. These feelings of "having been there before" appear from present evidence to throw direct light on the mechanism of orientation in time; the subject may have, at the critical moment of excitation, the feeling that he has gone through this particular experience before and that the surgeon is about to take some specific step. There is, in other words, evidence of time disorientation with its specific cerebral locus, and under conditions in which manifestly the patient has not been in that situation before.

Now the important thing for us, from this viewpoint, is the disorder in reality testing which appears: the subject feels as if all this had happened before, just as he feels, on direct excitation of a "memory center" in the temporal lobe, as if he were reliving an actual experience such as the one described on page 72. There is a disturbance in the ability to estimate his own position in time. It is not just a question of the expansion or contraction of time as we know it from the study of drug effects, such as those from hashish; rather, it is a radical shifting of the person to a different stance, a different point in the time flow. What is often most real in such experiences is denied by the kind of reality emphasized in the study of clock time by the experimental scientist. There are two or more time systems. William James has referred to this kind of double consciousness effect, and it has been rather elaborately studied from the pharmacological point of view.

All this seems to mean that on the screen of reality used constantly by the subject to check his own position, there may be memory-feedback failures, essentially like the visual-feedback failures mentioned above, and also the spatial and other orientation failures for which the proprioceptive system may be responsible. As Snyder and Pronko, and Kohler have shown, the subject with long experiences in an unreal visual world may feel almost violently certain as to what is real, although it is belied by other lines of evidence from his own sense organs and from those of others. The overwhelming conviction that one system of reality is real, and another less real or not real at all, seems intimately related to a time-space orientation process. We are not quite ready to say that there is a "center for reality testing" nor indeed, in somewhat more mystical language, to say that there is a "reality center." Rather, we are ready to say that reality as encountered may go through myriad qualitative and quantitative changes, as a result of tissue changes in the brain, and that it will be necessary to incorporate findings of this sort in our ultimate interpretation as to what man really does when he "makes contact with reality."

As we raise the question of "memory feedback versus effector feedback," we are reminded that the first evolutionary task of memory is to give information on the consequences of what we are doing, or are about to do. Painful memories are associated with hot stoves, and along with the conditioned avoidance response, there is the memory of the stove, a memory which may come back as we enter the door or as we sit in another part of the house. The memory may involve an image, vivid or vague, or it may involve only a "set," or a schema. We cannot here analyze its structure, but we must note that as behavior goes on, floods of memories in the form of anticipated consequences and related associated events play a continuous part in current activity. It is therefore quite correct to speak of memory feedback as a process by which our current acts bring back, not just knowledge of the immediate physical consequences, but knowledge of related events. The exteroceptive feedback of K. U. Smith and W. M. Smith (page 62) gives correct or incorrect guidance in acts depending upon time relations; in the same way, the experience of *déjà vu* suggest a timing fault with reference to the memory process — a mixed reality of present and past which cannot rationally exist.

As a matter of fact, we learn to duplicate clinical anomalies of this sort by the experimental process of intersecting one time with another, or intersecting time with a space dimension which does not belong to it. An extreme illustration is the commando device of World War II, somewhat similar to the brain-washing device reported in connection with the mainland Chinese techniques of remaking personality: the inquisitor finds a way of consistently denying or misrepresenting memories of the prisoner's past, his earlier or deeper convictions; skillfully and continuously a different past is fed in.

There is no mail; there are no visits to correct the impressions funneled in; and a large part of the past is successfully replaced with a pseudo-past which, in time, takes on the quality of reality, because it is consistent within itself and consistent with the immediate exteroceptive environment. Orwell's *1984* is an extrapolation from existing possibilities.

The question naturally arises whether, through a conditioning process, any act we carry out may give rise to memories which serve to control the next act to take place. From an examination of motor habits, like buttoning a coat or closing a snap, it would certainly appear that such control of memories by acts, and of further acts by memories, is a standard and normal part of adjustment to environmental requirements. The principle of hierarchical organization and of inhibition must, nevertheless, be remembered: memory may, so to speak, discharge upwards into more complex judgmental and imaginative processes, arresting effector processes. There is indeed good evidence that slight differences in memory pattern — the way we remember an important past situation — may determine whether we ruminate, inhibit, or change course, whether we take a new direction or give added impetus to what is already in course.

SUMMARY

In this chapter we have extended the discussion of the "reality" of the inner world by raising the question whether "knowledge" of interoceptive stimulation can lead to voluntary control over inner functions, such as that of the heart, heretofore thought to be beyond volitional control. While no empirical proof yet exists that permits an unequivocally affirmative answer, we have tried to show that in principle such inner, voluntary control is possible and that attempts to demonstrate it deserve serious attention. Then, from a slightly different perspective, we have sought to illuminate the vital role inner processes play in reality apprehension by citing the effects of stimulation of the neurophysiological substrate of memory upon orientation in time.

8

Criterion Tests of Reality

We have seen that learning plays a major role in the development of the individual's perceptual world — his construction of reality. We have assigned a central role to acts of attending — predicated upon a pattern of learned expectations — as the mechanism which from moment to moment constitutes the content and structure of reality. We have suggested that what the senses, thus steered by attention, make contact with emerges as "real" when it is part of a context directly represented by the organism's needs, or in terms of stimulus patterns, which are themselves ultimately related to needs, or when it is in a context of expected or required behavior.

We are ready now for the difficult question raised by the phenomenon of misperception, when ordinary reality testing fails and faulty interpretation of reality results and when doubt arises about the "reality" that has seemed to have been perceived.

Do the Senses Mediate Reality?

Classically, "reality" had to depend upon the test of action (the pragmatist's test, compare page 45), or the world of consistency of one's own impressions and formulations, or the test of interpersonal agreement or "consensual validation." A thing is real when it leads to successful predictions, or to our own internal conviction of consistency, or to social confirmation. From this viewpoint, error can arise from failure at one or more of these levels. *Illusion* may arise when the evidence of the senses is conflicting or conflicts with the judgment or thought, which, stepping down from a higher or general level, points to a failure in the ordinary reality-testing process.

What is of interest in these definitions is the implicit assumption that the senses ordinarily *mediate reality*, and that humans can quickly catch them by one or another of these three criteria if they fail to do their job. The truth, we are sure, is waiting there to be apprehended. The sense organs, conjoined and under control of effective *seeking* and *scanning* and abetted by criteria of practical tests as well as logical consistency, keep us in more or less constant and adequate contact with reality.

CULTURE AS A MEDIATOR OF REALITY

Now this is rather an extraordinary doctrine for anyone who studies the way things appear to men at different phases, in their success and failure, health and disease, youth and old age, and as they appear to different men in different periods and in different cultural areas. One of the very first things men must do if they are to live at all in society is to see things more or less as other men do, and if the sense organs and the higher processes of judgment and thought get very far from filling this requirement, men are slain or tortured or shut up in a physical sense, or "shut up" in a slightly more metaphorical sense. An extraordinary part of the energies of the group — especially of the women who regulate the introduction of the young into the accepted ways of life — consists of guiding them into a way of seeing, understanding, valuing, and accepting what is defined as the compellingly real. Xenophanes observed that snub-nosed races make their gods snub-nosed, and that athletes, like the Greeks themselves, made gods into athletes. The raw texture of the world may be much the same for us all, but there are demons inside motor boats if the culture requires it, as there are essentially human purposes in the mechanical process of nature in every society in which purpose is written into cosmic meaning.

It was the genius of Karl Mannheim to describe, under the term "the sociology of knowledge," the deep dependence of human thought forms, cognitive and affective, factual and valuational, upon the stuctured tone and ethos of society at a given time. Social reality, then, is thicker, so to speak, than the personal reality which comes from the little essence of one's daily experience, and the sociology of knowledge suggests a multidimensional "reality," in comparison with a rather flat formulation of "pragmatism" belonging to a period fifty years ago before the rise of the modern cultural sciences. We have a world perspective as well as a time perspective now beginning to dawn upon us, which make us realize to what an extraordinary degree the mind is not only a biological-evolutionary product, given to creatures who have sense organs and nervous systems like our own, but how deeply it is dyed in the rich hues of a culturally defined way of living, looking, feeling, and dreaming.

Within this system of ideas, working from the large to the small, one must deal with the specific reality-testing devices, which are accepted, class by class, community by community, within which even the world of time and space proves to depend upon social organization, upon the duties of the many different stations in life, and upon the requirements for structuring, in time and in space, what one has done, is doing, and is about to do.

We may say then that, in this view, reality is a matter of what is *allowed* to be real. In order to be real, a thing needs not only to break through into the life of the senses, but to be picked up by inner scanning; it has to get attention directed to it. It has to get over other hurdles having to do especially with holding attention, with marking, labeling, and bringing it into relation to central ego functions, such as values. If it fails in getting over any of these hurdles, it is likely to be a victim of

scotoma — a word meaning shadow, and by extension, meaning all that is excluded from sensory recognition.

REALITY AS THE "REQUIRED" PERCEPTUAL RESPONSE

Some types of perceptual "distortion" depend upon scotoma;
in other cases, a very good job of excluding evidence is done
without any scotoma whatever, simply by emphasis, accent,
and reorganization of the sensory materials given. A dramatic
illustration lies in the experiments of Kilpatrick. The subject
enters a large room within which he sees several small, more
or less cubical rooms, each of which has a peephole at an appropriate height to permit looking within it. He looks into the
first and sees the normal interior of a cube. He now has the
task, however, of throwing a rubber ball, which bounces about
from one wall to another within the little room, or of aiming
a flashlight at one point or another. Very rapidly what he
sees begins to change. The cube begins to disappear, the floor
to tip, one of the walls to slant. Within thirty or forty minutes
the typical observer begins to see a truncated, inverted
pyramid. The action and the context (as discussed above,
page 44) have changed the requirements of the situation. It
is only in a room having these tilts and slants that the ball
could behave as it has been seen to behave. The subject has
therefore apprehended "reality." He has see the room as it is!

Or has he? He has seen it as the cues require. The subject is now led to another little room, and looks through a
peephole into it. He sees a small room which, for him, is
plainly an inverted, truncated pyramid. So now, he tries his
reality test with the ball. But the ball bounces about in the
new room; the room loses its appearance as a truncated, inverted pyramid, and insists upon turning back again, a step at
a time, into the cube form seen previously.

The point is simply that the individual learned to see the
first room "as it really was," then carried over the naïve
perceptual habits, thus formed, to the *new* room. He saw the
new room in the light of the expectations so rapidly ingrained
in him; he saw it as a truncated, inverted pyramid. He saw

it as another "distorting room." But it was not any such thing; it was a normal cube-type room. Habits had been learned just as they are learned day by day, in such a way as to give a new meaning to experience as required by action.

Many who have read such experiments have inclined to the view that the subject will inevitably "get to the truth of the matter"; he will slowly rid himself of the illusory percepts and see things as they are. There will be a natural rightness, a natural realism involved in human perceptual capabilities. This belief springs from our deep conviction that after all we encounter the real. There is indeed some truth in this, but it calls for much more sophistication. Insofar as there are nail heads not properly painted over, or tiny cracks in the wood which admit the light, there may indeed be "give-away clues"; i.e., information which will clash with some of the misleading information, and will lead the subject back to reality. The fact is, however, that in the second experiment just described, the subject perceptually prefers the "*distorted*" or "untrue" impression on the basis of its actual visual merits, even though any errors in the creation of the room — cracks in wood, poorly painted nail heads, etc. — would actually work in the direction *opposite* to the reality the subject accepts. It is the practical test, the pragmatic test, that wins out in the competition. There are indeed countless instances in everyday life in which the person clings to errors (note some of the illusions on page 83) which have simply not been overwhelmed by contrary training effects. These experiments are interesting supplements to the principle described above (page 77) regarding the failure of any ultimate or absolute test of reality beyond the meaning test or the action test described above. Indeed, as McNamara has put it: "you can get either a progression towards reality or away from reality depending upon the way in which your experiment is built up." Kilpatrick's experiments demonstrate the use of the principle of functional organization in terms of the "requiredness" of one perceptual response rather than another; this requiredness is partly given by inherent structural necessity in the environment, partly by inherent structural necessity in the organism, and partly by experience in terms of both meaning and action.

REALITY AND INDIVIDUALITY

Philosophers insist that there is a world of logic which is not invalidated by the considerations urged here. We shall try to do justice to this point below (page 133). But the argument from perceptual self-checking or consensual validation does not easily lead to such a view. It leads rather to a study of reality testing in terms of the three principles just described, and therefore to the idea that *reality* is a term with *psychological meaning,* and is defined for each of us in terms of degrees of compatibility between specific evidence and the broader system of beliefs which have been set up as a criterion for individual living. Such individuality is subject always, of course, to the coercions of geography and culture within which individual adaptations occur.

9

Conflicting Evidence and How It Is Handled

As we learned from the Kilpatrick experiments, there may be a true clash between the two (or more) meanings of perceptual evidence. Reversible figures, like the Necker Cube shown in Figure 2, are a commonplace field of psychological inquiry, and many of the factors which favor an incorrect interpretation, not capable of consensual validation, are familiar icons of the laboratory. There are many cases in which either of two interpretations — as in this case — is right. We have emphasized cases in which the "wrong" interpretation is the one learned and "required."

Figure 2

83

The heart of the problem lies in the ways of handling the clash of evidence. Memory traces often say that it must be so; the fresh perceptual impact disagrees. Or, one sensory message disagrees with another. Proprioceptive feedback gives the lie to the exteroceptive report. There is much interest today in the contradiction in perceptual evidence that may be called "perceptual dissonance."

These experiences are usually, and perhaps always, instances in which there are mutually exclusive interpretations which are represented by mutually exclusive *expectations*. If my theory is anchored at one point, and all depends upon it, I shall not listen with "objectivity" to evidence that conflicts with it. Just as the "problem of error" is fatal to any absolute philosophical realism, so the fact of perceptual dissonance is, we think, absolute refutation of the doctrine that perception finds, resonates to, incorporates the one modality by which reality can be known. Perception is simply not that kind of peerless guide with whom none can compete in leading us in the reality direction. We shall see (page 85) that the issue between Protagoras and Plato is almost universally resolved today in favor of Plato; i.e., that the conceptual world of abstractions is free of the self-contradictions so manifest in the perceptual world. But the question remains open whether the unity of clear conceptualization bears the badge of truth more securely than does the testimony of perception. A primary psychological fact at this stage is the clash of evidence and the clash between expectations; the dual need for resolutions lies, first, in the fact of distress through conflict, and second, in the sheer need to live in terms of a choice between competing ways of acting.

We have indeed been forced more and more into recognition of a clash between modes of interpretation of reality: the clash is in the first instance a clash between perception and thought. Percepts warring with one another may give rise to the thought: which of the alternative percepts is "valid"? What is *really* there? Conflict is the mother of science. Percepts may also, however, engage in such sibling rivalry that thought is distracted and inhibited. Humanity has basically learned to believe, and firmly believes — as shown in philosophy, science, the law — that there is an order of consistency to be found by the thought process which is not found at the perceptual level. There is the possibility of clear abstractions, and there is the possibility that the fragments of evidence offered by perception may be interpreted at a higher level into a unity from which we may look back with serenity (or amusement) at the apparent contradiction — now no longer held to be a contradiction — between the perceptual evidences.

THE PRINCIPLE OF INHIBITION

Now this control of the lower process by a higher one is a clear instance of the general principle of inhibition, a clear reflection of the organic necessity that there shall somewhere be final integration, unity of response; it will have to be at the highest level because only here can unity of action be guaranteed. For us, "reality" is the integrated something which must exist there if we are to take into account all the scattered evidence, process it, and face it in terms of action. "Reality" is that which emerges after we have forced into reluctant agreement all perceptual evidences, knocked their heads together, sat upon them with a firm demand that all should agree. Often the belief which finally wins in such a contest proves to have taken the wind out of all competing evidences. Subsequent evidence may actually be rejected, or may be turned to the benefit of the accepted principles, just as the convert may passionately reject his former beliefs, and may regard each evidence previously accepted by him as proof of the perversity, the stupidity, the willfulness of his prior self. All future counterarguments may, as in the case of the suffering Job, serve only to intensify the solid certainty of one's final conviction.

Conflicting evidence may be rejected or suppressed by means of the "gating" process, which has received considerable attention in recent years. It will be recalled that

Hernández-Peón demonstrated that when a mouse is introduced into a hungry cat's field of vision, concomitant auditory
stimulation is "gated out" before it reaches cortical centers.
Similarly, Braatoy's patients employed proprioceptive input
from skeletal muscles to gate out painful memories.

Indeed, gating is a special case of the broad principle of
inhibition. Such gating, moreover, seems clearly to exemplify
a sub-principle that inhibitory processes from higher levels
to lower levels may supersede inhibition among components
of equal rank in a hierarchy. If there is a reality apprehension,
reality determination at the highest level, almost everything
must yield to it. The hysterical anesthesia and the anesthesia
of the hypnotized subject make far more convincing the
classical views that the martyr and the zealot may literally
feel no pain.

We find ourselves therefore in the midst of a company of
competing individual tendencies and groups of tendencies.
Under failure of integration, these tendencies could become a
crowd or a mob. But they normally manage, by some complex
process, to set up an oligarchic system in which a few tendencies agree more or less with one another for the sake of holding
power, and one theme — perhaps an integrated self-image, or
word, or just a perseverating tension system in the muscles —
holds authority at least through the period of decision. Genuine crises are infrequent, and often appear clinically as
failures of will, as total inaction, on the one hand, and as
explosive failures of impulse control, on the other.

The conception of the process of inhibition as the major
mode by which conflicts arising from the clash of contradictory
perceptual evidence or from unfulfilled expectations are resolved, also emphasizes that levels of reality are not given
simply in terms of "cognitive clearness." The perception, judgment, or self-image that finally achieves the status of "most
real," is not indeed the clearest among competitors but the
most strategic. Levels of reality are dimensions of personal
relevance and are fundamental in the definition of self and
life.

The Psychoanalytic System and Levels of Reality

The Freudian psychoanalytic system has taught us to think of the complexities of internal personality structure in dynamic terms, in terms of power or energy relationships among structural elements such as id, ego and superego. The psychoanalytic approach to the person involves studies of gating, studies of active selection and exclusion, of blocking, reinforcement — fresh, vital disentangling and reassembly in terms of the internal energies each component possesses.

The psychoanalytic system gives a prominent place to the conception of the real, but it is mostly in connection with the process of reality testing, and hardly at all toward a conception of *levels of reality or of unreality.* "Primary process," the earliest mode of reality testing and characteristic of infancy, is conceived as a process in which our wishes are converted through hallucination, delusion, or convenient daily belief into that which we need. Primary process is gradually and partially displaced by "secondary process," in which one delays the gratification of an impulse and takes a roundabout route in reaching out for the real. Secondary process and the concept of reality testing are conceived to be processes of emancipation from naïve shortcuts to gratification.

The real, then, is that which has to be accepted, has to be sought and worked through. To be sure, the psychoanalytic system regards evasion and distortion as fundamental and as a process that occurs because too many things are too real. But the legerdemain of scotoma and distortion is not viewed as ever completely derealizing the components. The turning away and the isolation process establish a sort of "pretend" unreality. The process of "denial" is the only one of the ten mechanisms described by Anna Freud which even pretends to achieve complete *rejection of the reality* of a threatening situation. In the psychoanalytic view the internal battle relates rather rarely to denial, to the wholesale shunting aside of information as unreal, to which our conception of levels of reality as structurally and dynamically prominent give a more important place.

Often what we regard as the *real* during normal internal contests for power is that for which sacrifices are made. Up to a certain point the degrees of value determine the position in the reality hierarchy. When once there is consolidation of internal control or some sort of clear hierarchical system, the commitment, the movement towards such consolidation, acts to define the real. "It must be real if I am giving so much to this." Or the real is, after all, that which is one's own. The Shakespeare line, as usual, states it well: "A poor thing, but mine own."

But there is more than an oligarchy. There is a true center. There has to be a center, as much within the person as within the unsettled affairs of states. This was James's "pontifical cell," a metaphor, of course, but a useful one. This moving organizing center is the "master cell" to which Masefield refers:

> If I could get within this changing I,
> This ever altering thing which yet persists,
> Keeping the features it is reckoned by,
> While each component atom breaks or twists,
> If wandering past strange groups of shifting forms,
> Cells at their hidden marvels hard at work,
> Pale from much toil, or red from sudden storms,
> I might attain to where the Rulers lurk.
> If, pressing past the guards in those grey gates,
> The brain's most folded, intertwisted shell,
> I might attain to that which alters fates,
> The King, the supreme self, the Master Cell;
> Then, on Man's earthly peak I might behold
> The unearthly self beyond, unguessed, untold.

DENIAL OF REALITY AND PERSONALITY ORGANIZATION

The blocking of messages is seldom a wholly local and specific matter. The skills of buffering are capable of extension through "response generalization"; e.g., the same skill will apply to new kinds of threats. There is also much "stimulus generalization" in the interpretation of threats and distasteful systems of all sorts; we view a threat as we have viewed others which resemble it. There are, to meet new threats, "buffer systems" like the buffer system of the blood, often organized in depth, so that when the outer defenses are taken, a second or a third line of defense may be called into action (compare Ashby and the construction of an "ultra-stable" system organized to deal with highly generalized classes of adversities). Such general buffer systems are constructed against information in its own right or through its conditioned stimulus values, which stands for that which might breach the defenses. The "signal anxiety" of the psychoanalyst is just one of a variety of these mechanisms. There are probably other aversive response systems, such as the disgust system, which operate as the anxiety system operates.

Such systems may come near the apex of personality organization. A person may be organized around his buffering processes. Sometimes he may be the highly rigid defensive excluder of information, or this response may in turn be organized either in terms of passive resistance or in active onslaught against threats, a chip-on-the-shoulder system which anticipates and meets in advance all threats which are likely to arise. The "hyperalertness" of the paranoid who scans the external environment actively for information consonant with his delusional construction of reality and also for signs of expected danger vividly exemplifies this response. The central point, as far as the issue of reality is concerned, is that in such cases it simply is not wanted. Reality contains too many things that might lead to trouble, and levels of reality somewhere on the lower end of our scale — things that might be real but that we would rather not think about — are important parts of the operating basis for life. Mark Antony, speaking over the body of Caesar, knew how to organize in depth against information; so did Iago.

LEARNING TO REJECT INFORMATION

Ordinarily such extreme maneuvers are hardly necessary. One may set up buffer systems through teaching a person where and how to direct his attention, with a view to the establishment of habits of attending which will certainly block the advent of useful information. What the experimenter does, tongue in cheek, is to guide the subject to various ways of assimilating information which are nevertheless likely to trap him into inefficient habits. The "left" study of J. F. Santos and his collaborators exemplifies processes by which brief, but vigorous and effective training of attention can buffer information, or can welcome it in. Santos trained several groups of subjects to detect the word LEFT (white against a black background as shown below) by differing methods of training.

Figure 3

Among his subjects was a group required to practice reversing figure and ground with a variety of practice material. Another group received no training other than to identify a series of nonsense forms and code them by appropriate number. The practice in figure-ground reversal had by far the greatest value in relation to finding the hidden word, practice in coding much less. We may conclude therefore that the subject who is taught to *code* small details of information is unwittingly trained into misdirection of attention, while the subject trained in *reversal from white to black* learns a readiness which makes him highly effective in seeing the organized white space which represents the word *left*. One can thus systematically and quantitatively prepare the individual either to accept or to reject, to use or to avoid using the information streams forever flowing towards him.

The implication is that error would be reduced and that the proportion of higher levels of reality contact would be increased insofar as the individual learns to take note of his own errors in information processing. This would be a special case of the general principle of "knowledge of results." But from the viewpoint developed here, training through knowledge of results is partly cognitive restructuring and partly reinforcement through the more satisfying character of the information processing when on the way towards a desired goal. The McNamara experiment alluded to earlier involving training subjects to estimate the lengths of horizontal lines, and giving them "social reinforcement" in terms of praising or belittling the performance, leads to a tendency to overshoot or undershoot respectively in estimates of lines. This change in judging habits is transferred even when judging in the vertical rather than the horizontal direction, and when judging in terms of arbitrary units (not the familiar inches ordinarily used) in this specific task. In other words, the subjects carry out some transfer from one task to another, involving to some degree different movements of the eyes, and the feedback may produce either increased or decreased error.

This is one of the many lines of evidence brought out elsewhere in the course of our argument to suggest that there is no *necessary* movement towards reality as a result of more commerce with the physical realities of sensory presentations. The same lines may be more accurately or less accurately judged depending upon the way in which they serve the subject's needs. In this instance, the need to be correct from the point of view of the experimenter takes precedence over any ultimate or absolute truth need or veridical tendency that may exist in the subject. Those Gestalt presentations, which suggest that there is inevitably a movement of response in the direction of isomorphic harmony with the stimulus pattern, will seldom be useful to the type of analysis presented here.

The Automatic Correction of Error

However, there is certainly a level at which the correction of error is automatic. Homeostatic mechanisms keep body temperature or blood acidity, for example, from going "too far" in terms of some standard or norm built into the body. Such mechanisms, of course, appear at the inorganic level, and those which function to maintain homeostatic balance are based, ultimately, upon physico-chemical mechanisms of a high order of complexity to give them the "ultra-stable" form we mentioned above (page 89). The correction of error through feedback is simply a special case of these generalized adaptive mechanisms. The correction of error is involuntary long before we reach the level at which it can become voluntary. At the voluntary level we are dealing with free play, back and forth, until a limit on either side is reached, and a swing back occurs toward the norm. In fact, sine wave or simple harmonic motion is the typical expression of movement accelerating in the middle of the range, becoming slower towards the extreme, and then, after a reversal, freshly accelerating towards the mean. This is what happens in the movement of a pendulum, and is more or less useful as a key to what happens as a man, on a very warm day in a very cold wind in the mountains, puts on a sweater and takes it off; first he is too hot, and then he is too cold.

We have, however, with one rush carried ourselves beyond the simplest physical or organic processes; indeed, we have carried ourselves all the way to a voluntary process. There is a rich spectrum of possibilities from this autonomic adjustment of body temperature all the way on up to rational inner debate on a high issue, and the ego is always ready to come in. Transfer the situation from the trifling one on the mountain path to that of a man standing before an audience of many thousands, deciding whether he will try that rather corny story or not, alternating like the "schematic sowbug" between the image of himself as quite a wag and the image of himself as a stupid bore who has overtaxed the patience of his audience. There is then the "voluntary correction of error" as a sort of capstone or extreme case of the general principle of more or less homeostatic alternation from too much to too little of a particular kind of response.

Both Helson and Piaget have helped us with new concepts and new terminology with reference to this perpetual adaptive process, which goes on at every level from the profoundly unconscious to the precisely and expressly conscious. There may be a movement of the organism just far enough to bring the stimulus world into the existing pattern — this Piaget calls "assimilation" — or there may be an outward movement of the organism to engulf the situation, called by him "accommodation." It is our thesis that some accommodation is bound to occur through sheer physical proximity, through flow of matter and energy as in the convection and conduction of warmth through tissues and through the ambient air or liquid, and that much more accommodation will occur as a result of the learning process. To pursue our example, our mountaineer, by wearing heavy clothing in winter or light clothing in the summer, will adjust his warmth needs by preventing the escape of warmth, in the one case, and by accelerating it, in the other. There will, therefore, be acts of almost continuous accommodation of one part of the body to another, and of the body as a whole to the environment. But as follows from the principles in perceptual development, there will likewise be modification of the properties of each new stimulus by the Gestalt principle of "membership character," and by virtue of Herbart's dynamics of the "apperceptive mass" (page 32), there will be complex adjustments of each new value to the system of values already organized within. Thus by another route we reach the same principle, namely, automatic self-correction, as the limiting pole for a complex adaptive process.

INFORMATION THEORY AND ERROR REDUCTION

It is possible to formulate, from the viewpoint of "information theory," the quantitative relations between various forms of information input and the corresponding reduction of error. This is important from an engineering and data processing viewpoint, but it will probably turn out to have very much broader psychological implications. It is likely that in the effort to restate the process of communication, in highly abstract quantitative forms, and the attempt to organize education grade by grade and process by process, in terms of feedback theory, there may be a restatement of the modalities by which the individual may approximate to a working truth or reality through some "law of least action." It is indeed possible likewise that each social group, or even humanity at large, may find an individualized path leading towards the reality based upon the specifics and the generalities of such use of feedback. It would ill behoove an effort of the present sort to belittle the enormous possibilities which may come our way as a result of these rapid changes.

Yet from the point of view of the psychology of man as far as we understand him today, there is a very large dimension missing in such an approach, a dimension starting with some elementary data of motivation, and extending to a study of the way in which motivation sensitizes us to certain kinds of data processing, including data processing relating to the very nature of the motivation itself. Feedback of this sort could be of huge importance. In giving emphasis above to the variety of ways in which conflicting evidence is resolved and to the several mechanisms by which error is reduced, or becomes real, we have neglected that coherence and unity which is a modal aspect of all individual experience. Therefore, we turn now to an examination of the role of the self, as the central perceptual system and as the persistent coordinator of the experience of reality.

10

The Role of the Self

There are two reasons why the problem of the real and of reality testing enters a new phase with the first reference to the self. First, there is a dynamic significance everywhere in the fact that things are not just perceived; they are perceived in relation to the self. Things are usually not just remembered; they are remembered in terms of a place, an act, and a feeling that they belong to the self. Things are not just expected or anticipated; they are activities in which the self will be involved. All reality therefore has a self-reference. The second reason lies in the fact that the heightening of the sense of reality and the heightening of the sense of self are intimately related. Experiences of depersonalization and derealization are often referred to in interchangeable terms. The concept and the methods applicable to training in the abrogation of self-awareness, such as hypnosis, yoga, and the psychedelic drugs, sometimes produce the strange sense that all is unreal, or on the contrary, a sense that all is intensely real at a level at which we are not very sure how useful the language epithets "real" and "unreal" are. At any rate, "self" and "real" are two terms that seem to pulsate or whirl in our diction. They refuse

95

to stand pat. They are involved, one with the other. We cannot talk about the real without talking about the self. This becomes especially clear when we encounter not *loss* of reality or *loss* of selfhood, but a tremendous *intensification* of both in various types of spontaneously or deliberately inculcated awareness of reality. Some people, wishing to drown the awareness of reality, drink; others drink to apprehend a reality not otherwise obtainable to them. William James reminds us that nitrous oxide may give an enormous intensity of affirmation. The recent collection of contemporary case studies by Marghanita Laski yields dozens of examples of intense realization along with enhancement of self-awareness. The following experience, described by the American poet Bayard Taylor, will convey this feeling tone.

It was, perhaps, an hour past midnight, along the foothills of the Nevadas, when, as I lay with open eyes gazing into the eternal beauty of the night, I became conscious of a deep murmuring sound, like that of a rising wind. I looked at the trees; every branch was unmoved — yet the sound was increased until the air of the lonely dell seemed to vibrate with its burden. A strange feeling of awe and expectancy took possession of me. Not a dead leaf stirred on the boughs; while the mighty sound — choral hymn, sung by ten thousand voices — swept down over the hills, and rolled away like a retreating thunder over the plain. It was no longer the roar of the wind. As in the wandering prelude of an organ melody, note trod upon note with slow, majestic footsteps, until they gathered to a theme, and then came in the words chanted by an immeasurable host: *Vivant terrestria!* . . .

Suddenly, far overhead in the depths of the sky, rang a single, clear piercing voice of unnatural sweetness. Beyond the reach of human organs, or any human instrument, its keen alto pierced the firmament like a straight white line of electric fire. . . . It vibrated slowly into the fragment of a melody, unlike any which had ever reached my ear — long undulating cry of victory and joy, while the words: *Vivat Coelum!* were repeated more and more faintly while the voice slowly withdrew . . . then all was silent.

The intimacy of the relation between self and sense of the real are demonstrated with equal drama in the following subjective account of a mental patient's experience of depersonalization.

> It [the feeling of being unreal] makes each day assume a magnitude and importance that would not ordinarily be expected of it. Little things that could be thought of as small, when one has the will to decide big and small and to put things in their relative positions as much as is possible, become huge and assume frightening proportions. It is as if everything that is done during the day is done automatically and, then, examined by the feeling that would have been put into the act, had it been committed in a reasonably normal way. Just as the Church was rent apart by schisms, the most sacred monument that is erected by the human spirit, i.e., its ability to think and decide and will to do, is torn apart by itself. Finally, it is thrown out where it mingles with every other part of the day and judges what it has left behind. Instead of wishing to do things, they are done by something that seems mechanical and frightening, because it is able to do things and yet unable to want to or not to want to. All the constructive healing parts, that could be used healthily and slowly to mend an aching torment, have left, and the feeling that should dwell within a person is outside, longing to come back and yet having taken with it the power to return. Out and in, are probably not good terms though, for they are too black and white and it is more like gray. It is like a constant sliding and shifting that slips away in a jelly-like fashion, leaving nothing substantial and yet enough to be tasted, or like watching a movie based on a play and, having once seen the play, realizing that the movie is a description of it and one that brings back memories and yet isn't real and just different enough to make all the difference.

If a grand debate were set up between those who affirm that the self stands in the way of the apprehension of reality and those who affirm that self-enhancement and reality-enhancement are two phases of the same process, one could cite equally powerful advocates of these two positions. Clearly, we must look more closely for a useful definition of self and of its role in the contact with the real.

Self as the Central Perceptual System

We noted earlier that sensory data are forged into meaningful integrations called percepts, and that they have a dynamic exactly such as Herbart supposed, an internal dynamic or cohesion, resisting disturbance, and an external dynamic, involving outer energy relations. At times these are simple push-and-pull relations, at times the more integrative and disruptive, or consonant and dissonant relationships. From this point of view the self is the richest and most complex of the perceptual systems. It is highly flexible, but it is also "ultra-stable." It is attended to a good deal of the time; it controls behavior even when it is not attended to.

Like other perceptual systems, but to an extraordinarily high degree, it has the capacity to push other perceptual units aside, apparently because the love, fear, disgust, and other affectively toned attitudes directed towards it are of such enormous force. Actually it is the dynamic of love of the image of one's own body, the sound of one's own voice, etc. (compare page 62) which makes the self stand out so very prominently. It is not only *the thing that is there most of the time* in all our waking hours, or years — "overlearned," one might say — but it is dynamically the primary center with reference to which other things are measured ("Man is the measure of all things"). It is also the perceptual unity most directly related to what we are carrying out, and therefore has almost unlimited and continuous reinforcement from other activities. It is the center of life, except in those rare instances of devotion to another person greater than devotion to one's own self ("Greater love has no man than this"), or those cases of supernal dedication like the Spartans and Thespians who died at Thermopylae.

This means that the self, by virtue of the cathexis, the investment in it, wins out in most competitions with other investments however precious. This is the case not solely because of some superficial role of daily social reinforcement, however important that may be, but because of the central position of the self-image in the world of reality. From this point of view, the whole problem of voluntary attention we considered above (page 41), takes on a new light; for that which controls attention is, in large measure, that system of deep strong forces which stands ready forever to defend and enhance the self.

But one attends not only in order to defend oneself, to enhance oneself, but to keep the world adequate in terms of the basic requirements of the self. Voluntary attention is not just a kind of attention dependent upon the striped musculature such as the external eye muscles; rather, the striped muscles, whatever they may be in all the adjustive systems of the body, are perpetually at work steering attention in directions which are salutary in terms of the self, that is, response to the deep gratifications which come from all that favors the self or wards off threats against it. Voluntary attention is self-generated. It is not only concerned with the self a large part of the time, but it derives from self. There seems here to be a shortcut into the problem of what is real in this world: that is real which commands voluntary attention.

WISH FULFILLMENT AND THE REALITY PRINCIPLE

There is indeed a sharply etched reality also in the objects which threaten the self by hinting that they will take away its gratifications, or that they will enhance the things that do violence to it. There are two familiar explanations of the extravagant level of reality ordinarily attached to the noxious or self-defeating, despite the need of us all for good news only. First, in short-range terms we have to see the bad sharply and clearly; we have to give it maximum reality status in order to keep it away from the self. Certainly in the matter of painful memories as well as painful percepts and anticipations, this is a good working principle. But a second, broader principle is at work: the fact that we need that dependable safety which comes from an all-around comprehensive acceptance of the environment for the sake of the adequacy of our contact with the world. Petty failures are unimportant, but to develop a basic stance in life which denies the evidence of stress and threat is the same as to become "unrealistic" in one's own eyes as well as in those of others. In other words, there is a threat to self-esteem if one allows the principle of "wishful thinking" and of affective control of perception and reasoning too large an area of freedom. Voluntary attention then may be conceived as a searchlight looking mostly for the good, but like the binoculars sweeping for icebergs, maximally sensitized to that which is most dangerous.

A fundamental thesis of psychoanalysis, confirmed by much experimental evidence, is that there is grave confusion in the little child between the desirable and the real, and that only slowly, and with much distress in the learning process, does one come to the sober reflection that the wished-for is unreal and the ardently-to-be-rejected is the real. It does not take masses of experimental evidence to convince us in general that wishful perceiving, remembering, imagining, and thinking tend not only to bring us pleasant melody, but that they do actually deceive us not uncommonly; they sing siren songs we have known to be deceptive, but which we never fully learn to reject. Voluntary attention is then guided by two masters: a reality principle and a wish-fulfilling or primary process principle. Training in reality seeking must, in some measure, be training to accept the former rather than the latter.

But we are writing as if voluntary attention and the whole massive role of the self which lies behind it were directed mainly to getting a consistent, practical, dependable view of the outer world. It is to almost exactly the same degree directed to getting a consistent and workable view of the *inner* world. One checks forever what one sees inside against other things to be seen inside, and any and all of these are to be checked against what is seen outside. The memory processes stand on the middle of the bridge, derived as they are both from prior exteroceptive and prior interoceptive experience, inclining this way and that, now towards an emphasis upon fresh exteroceptive information — the seeking of *new* information — and at times asking whether one's appraisal of what is within is actually sound, correct, in harmony with what one deeply knows to be true. Here lies much of the problem of objectivity, and of conscience. This is a way of saying that there is the same struggle towards compactness, integration, internal consistency, and ultimate verification in the case of material within, as in the case of material without.

SELF-CONSISTENCY

This is close to the theme beautifully developed twenty-three years ago by Prescott Lecky in *Self Consistency: A Theory of Personality,* a series of essays full of homely, everyday wisdom relating to the perceptual struggle to keep the self-image well defined, internally consistent, and free of conflict. Lecky believed that the problems of normal adjustment consist very largely of finding a way to belittle the conflicting evidence which tries to raise its minority voice against the major forces of one's daily experience, and strove to show that it is not so much the good that one seeks for oneself as the self-consistent self-portrait.

There is much to be said in honor of Lecky's vigorous pursuit of the theme. However, he seems to have overlooked the fact that when the self-image is a source of distress, one may pitifully crave that inconsistent word of approval or affection which enhances the self-image, while actually making it less consistent; he seems to have overlooked the fact that self-consistency can be either sought or feared, depending upon whether the conflicting evidence raises or lowers the level of self-esteem.

But even so, central importance must be assigned to the doctrine of self-consistency as a tool for the understanding of the perceptual memory and thought dynamics of civilized man, overwhelmed as he is by cross-cultural and scientific-technological information about himself often incompatible with what comes to him from the deep tradition of his culture, and often representing a crossroads of conflicting messages regarding his worth. Self-consistency is one form of general perceptual cognitive consistency, and since we have taken the

view that such consistency is of profound importance in finding the real, we shall logically have to take the position that
self-consistency is a major component in the anchoring and
structuring of this broader system of consistent outlook.

The issues defined by Lecky are beautifully developed by
Erik Erikson in a series of volumes and essays in which the
conception of "ego identity" is developed against a background of cross-cultural studies of American Indian tribes,
Russians, Yale freshmen, submarine crews, German adolescents
in the Hitler era, disturbed California four-year-olds, the
turbulent young Martin Luther, and the prophetic Mahatma
Gandhi. The full-fledged evaluation of the process of discovering and holding on to oneself is integrated within a sensitive
conceptual system belonging, in its roots, to classical Freudian
psychoanalysis, but richly cultivated in the atmosphere of
psychoanalytic ego psychology, and particularly in a cross-
cultural psychology enriched by much observation and much
profound reflection upon what it is that man conceives himself to be. Ego identity becomes a richer conception than
"self-image" largely because of the overtones of cross-cultural
comparison and the undertones of psychoanalytic depth psychology. The issue, from the present writers' point of view,
is enriched, not challenged by these considerations. The real,
we would say as we read Erikson, is not merely that which
is demanded by the requirements of the self-image, but it is
that which is demanded by the requirements of ego identity.

As we watch our colleagues, concerned as they are with the
clinical or the experimental disentanglement of complicated
predilections and self-deceptions, we never cease to wonder
how little they see regarding their own self-deceptions, and
regarding the "idol of the den," and "idol of the clan"; members of each discipline fail to see the characteristic scotoma of
the group, the class, the profession to which we belong.
Further, the era of history, the cultural — especially the
scientific, industrial, technical — society has made so profound
a mark upon us that there is no chance of seeing it. As Law-
rence Frank so well said: "The last thing that a fish could
become aware of would be water." Or as John Useem

pointed out after serving as administrator of a Pacific Island group, American army officers can quickly learn an anthropological point of view, and learn to understand the conflicting cultural patterns of the different native groups; what they find it impossible to learn is to look at and perceive the American culture of which they are a part. The most violent affront to reality is not the wishful thinking, the distortion of the frightened or praise-hungry man, but the deep rejection of information which could, in any fundamental sense, damage the self or the beloved group in which the self has its shape and meaning.

Thus, "self-deception" is not a matter of little duels fought out with little weapons along the banks of a great stream of august reality to which most reasonable people most of the time conform. It is rather a major code of life, an apparently necessary code for the maintenance of the order which culture and which the family and individual have arrived at. It is a passive process when passivity will serve, but much of the time activity will serve better. Those processes of active, attentive exploration, considered above under the terms "seeking" and "scanning," apply also to the process of finding what is deeply acceptable to the self, and rejecting that which threatens it.

It takes hard work to keep the disturbing components from being accepted as real. A perpetual rearguard action must be maintained against the past, and an advance guard action against the future. Much of the strain of "modern life" is surely the strain of the unceasing effort to see the self both as consistent and as good in a cultural matrix in which precious friends disagree with one another and with the family, and in which little areas of ego autonomy conflict with parental and community norms. Moreover, there is conflict because of our conflict — "kicking ourselves because we kick ourselves" — and a reluctance to admit that conflict is there at all.

Recourse is then taken to a higher level process, making use of the whole organized resources of those drives which are invested in the self-image, those definitions of life in which the self is consistent and the proper arbiter of reality. This requires a "gating" process similar to the gating described above, but now organized in terms of a full-dress battle royal between our strongest inner tendencies and those magisterial forces which, organized around the self, cannot accept the terms of a competitor.

In his novel, *The Fall*, which is in some sense an autobiography of modern man in the Western world, Albert Camus' protagonist, struggling to achieve a "realistic" image of himself, speaks eloquently to this point:

> I have to admit it humbly, *mon cher compatriote*, I was always bursting with vanity. I, I, I is the refrain of my whole life, which could be heard in everything I said. I could never talk without boasting, especially if I did so with that shattering discretion that was my specialty. It is quite true that I always lived free and powerful. I simply felt released in regard to all for the excellent reason that I recognized no equals. I always considered myself more intelligent than anyone else, as I've told you, but also more sensitive and more skillful, a crack shot, an incomparable driver, a better lover. Even in the fields in which it was easy for me to verify my inferiority — like tennis, for instance, in which I was but a passable partner — it was hard for me not to think that, with a little time for practice, I would surpass the best players. I admitted only superiorities in me and this explained my good will and serenity. When I was concerned with others, I was so out of pure condescension, in utter freedom and all the credit went to me: my self-esteem would go up a degree.
>
> Along with a few other truths, I discovered these facts little by little in the period following the evening I told you about. Not all at once nor very clearly. First I had to recover my memory. By gradual degrees I saw more clearly, I learned a little of what I knew. Until then I had always been aided by an extraordinary ability to forget. I used to forget everything, beginning with my resolutions. Fundamentally, nothing mattered. War, suicide, love, poverty got my attention, of course, when circumstances forced me, but a courteous, superficial attention. At times, I would pretend to get excited about some cause foreign to my daily life. But basically I didn't really take part in it except, of course, when my freedom was thwarted. How can I express it? Everything slid off — yes, just rolled off me.

The battle is usually "won," and the self-image somehow maintained. However, there is at times a vague awareness that something is wrong. There may be sleeplessness, restlessness, a need for drugs, compliments, excitement to keep the accusing voice of self-disesteem from entering into clear awareness. Sometimes suspension on a knife-edge results in a sudden reversal of structure, and that which has been rejected and made to play the part of the unreal comes driving back in a whirlwind, and we encounter what Janet called "memories which are too real." For the most part this great overwhelming reversing process does not occur. For most men most of the time, the adage of Nietzsche seems to suffice: "I did it, said my memory. I could not have done it, said my pride, and in the end my memory yielded."

THE SELF AND COGNITIVE CONTROLS

The controls just described are habitual, affect-laden controls belonging to what we have called the self-system. They are not altogether independent, however, of "cognitive controls," devices described by G. S. Klein, Riley Gardner, H. J. Schlesinger, P. S. Holzman, and others, to define the individual styles of structuring the perceived world, the world remembered, thought about, imagined in a way which organizes, classifies, and makes sense out of the stimulus world in accordance with some personal idiom of interpretation. Objecting to the conception that affects, instincts, or impulses have a relatively free hand in controlling what will be accepted and what will be rejected from the stimulus complex acting upon us, and what will therefore control the swing of the rather homeostatic relation to environmental pressures, they undertake to define the huge and consistent individual differences which enable one individual to exclude what another cannot exclude, or to make fine distinctions when another can only make coarse distinctions in the same cognitive situation. Here they have a place for both blind and unaware modes of differentiation, integration, emphases, attention, predilections for contrast or assimilation, etc., and also for the establishment of different ground rules which permit one person to go to a higher level before decisions are made, while another prefers to remain at a lower, simpler, or more homeostatic level. Cognitive controls then are ingrained and consistent ways of regulating the impact of information as decisions are made. There is room in the theory for cognitive controls operating within a "conflict-free ego sphere," that is, providing for idiosyncrasies in the way in which perceptual, judgmental cognitive issues are handled. There is room also for the manner in which instinctual or autistic components are allowed to enter the theater of cognitive interplay. The theory of cognitive controls is a rich conceptualization of the personal idiom of perceiving, remembering, and thinking — recognizing both the rather coercive role of stimulus organization in its own right, and also the rather coercive role of internal systematic predispositions tending towards some sort of issue to be taken, some sort of duel to be established between the outer and the inner pressures (compare Rapaport, page 52).

PART

TWO

11

The Demand for the Real

The demons of self-deception, of which we made so much earlier, can at times be altogether exorcized. Somehow in the midst of fretful denial or extravagant self-adulation some small, clear voice demands the restoration of order, sanity, common sense. How can this happen? What is this reassertion of the real, this fresh reawakening to the cold and impersonal reality which had been nearly smothered by the delusional system fed in self-esteem? What possible dynamics can we find for the search of reality which throws pride, prejudice, and neurotic self-protection to the winds?

DETERMINANTS OF REALITY SEEKING

We believe the process is quite complex, and that the half-dozen factors we have struggled to develop, even when used in combination, will prove insufficient to do justice to the subtleties of this reality-seeking process. But we can make a preliminary inventory. The process is certainly: (1) an expression of curiosity; (2) a shortcut to practical advantage; (3) the reassertion of ego and superego against the more primitive or infantile primary process thinking; (4) a step to regain one's position with the social group by accepting the truth for which they — our social environment — stand; (5) an instance of reversal of perspective such as we saw earlier with the Necker Cubes, or a case of figure-ground reversal based on satiation or boredom; (6) but at times, it is a fairly pure operant (page 41). Having tried everything else, we try giving the situation a fresh look. (7) Certainly there is some of Sokolov's principle of pressure to reduce the gap between the inner model and the outer, or more broadly, the struggle towards achievement of an isomorphism of the inner and outer worlds, sheer strain or pressure in the sense of the exteroceptively challenging and inviting, all that it shares with the little inner "homunculus" isomorphic with it.

By whatever mode it is achieved, it is this process of self-correction that offers the core possibility for greater human reality contact, greater penetration of realities, and the potentialities which may become realized. It is the recognition, as William James said, that there is "always more," outgrowing the bonds of present self-limitation for the apprehension of present reality, and the developing of *openness* upon which the germinal — or not yet germinal — potentialities for new reals may come into existence. Just as we saw, with reference to generalized consequences of proprioceptive feedback (p. 64) so we find here, in more general terms, that progressive transfer and generalization to wider modes of apprehension may be possible.

Perhaps, as Berlyne suggests, this is a matter of increasing arousal-alerting activation. One might think here of a very generalized physiological or biochemical increase in arousal level, like the strychninization that Sherrington described as having a generalized overall facilitating effect upon the central nervous system functions. In fact, it is even possible that the affirmation during nitrous oxide described above (p. 96) or the "wild surmise" of the climber of high peaks, or the mystic sense of "unutterable revelation" may all be connected with this kind of reality resonance — and not only with the real which can be independently shown to be real by other, more sober methods, but with the real which newly comes into existence as evolution goes on.

There may then be an increasingly generalized sensitization

to the real, both in the sense of increased motivation or "love of the real," and in the sense of movement towards greater discriminating power, ultimately greater perceptual skill in making such contacts. It is likely that the development of such increasing skills will depend upon the use of all the help from contemporary learning theory in the generalization of these feedback skills, of discriminative skills generally, and also upon the discovery of devices controlled from without or from within, by which the reality hunger and the reality contact skill can be intensified.

DISCOVERY AND DISCIPLINE

But Aristotle's principle of the golden mean is relevant here. It has long been held against the ecstatic and the mystic that he is very sure, but not sure what he is sure about, and it is certainly true that many of the ectasy-producing and intoxicating devices long cherished by mankind have very little content for the guidance of daily life. One suspects that a sense of proportion may literally need to accompany the basic reality yearning, otherwise a tendency may develop to overshoot. One suspects that some of the extravagances of the modern psychedelic movement may lie precisely in the delicious sense of unlimited discovery without the discipline involved in developing the capacity to use the available feedbacks. In a society like ours, where guilt and self-blame are such highly standardized devices for cutting us back to the norm, it is likely that extravagant use of all the devices mentioned in this book for sensory enrichment, development of sensory and perceptual, judgmental, and thinking skills — especially in the use of feedbacks — and the use of physiological techniques from hatha yoga through progressive relaxation and hypnosis to psychedelic drugs, may lead to feeling of guilt when a little pocket of emptiness is entered. This too should not be exaggerated, for in most cases it is not really an exaggerated craving for reality that produces the excesses, but an exaggerated sense of well-being, specifically, a sense of self-enhancement, a sense of importance and goodness, and lovability of the self. At least at this writing it is not known whether a pathological reality-craving exists, and whether, if it exists, it can, all by itself, produce the revulsion and self-accusation so familiar in the case of extravagant boasts of knowledge. For most human beings most of the time, extravagant self-accusation is not the typical response. It is the unusual, the specially sensitive, the especially conscientious member of the cult group that is likely to attract attention.

REINFORCEMENT OF REALITY SEEKING

We think some sort of a case has been made for the possibility of developing a generalized reality-craving, serving a wide variety of secondary goals, yet centered in the delight in both perceptual and higher level contact with the world of which we are a part. Typically, one will achieve this habit of reality seeking and reality testing by fits and starts. Like other habits it will be acquired partly on a random and piecemeal basis, partly by the consolidation of simpler habits into more complex ones, partly by the joy, the special reinforcement that comes from higher level achievement, partly through the recognition given by others and the social reinforcement used, and partly by the restructuring of the self and the personality as a whole so that this reality urge becomes a central or core component in the total structure. Insofar as the correction of errors enters into the total process, we seem to be on familiar territory, in the sense that this is a component in all learning. The unsuccessful components in a complex skill are dropped out. But in keeping with the evidence of recent decades we believe that reward is, for the most part, more effective than punishment. It is not in stubbing one's toes on a tough unreality, or a plainly bad reality-seeking technique, that the chief learning lies. Rather, the main driving force is that which comes from the positive reinforcement of the satisfactions, the self-enhancements that follow. Reality seeking can therefore become habitual not only at the segmental level, but at the level of a highly generalized attribute, a quality of the person as a person.

12

Reality Seeking: The Enterprise of Mankind

For the most part, the individual human being we have been considering has been facing the world as if, so to speak, there were only one of him. Though we have referred to the social aspects of man's life on numerous occasions, we have assumed that each man individually makes his own cosmic contacts. This view serves us no longer. We shall have to pay a little more attention to the fact that reality is socially defined — defined by a cultural tradition, and by a specific human group in which one grows. The term "reality" is itself socially defined, and the criteria of the real are established while the infant is still battling out a number of distinctions that must be made between the expected things that happen, and the expected things that do not happen.

THE SOCIALIZATION OF REALITY SEEKING

We would anticipate, from this viewpoint, that failure to accept the reality defined by the group would be taken very seriously. It would lead to severe pressures on the little individual to accept the definition of the real offered to him, notably when his fantasies follow in a direction satisfying to himself, as in the autistic child, or when he enjoys the make-believe world enough to live in it, and populate it with his own rich creations to a point where this interferes with his understanding or his compliance with injunctions. From this point of view there must be, sometimes, in everyone's life, and often in the lives of a few people, instances in which a specially vigorous effort must be made to insist upon reality first at the behavioral level, and then later at the inner level which is assumed to exist in dreams and fantasy.

The psychotherapist's approach may involve a simple demonstration, a calling of attention to stimuli or responses not previously noted. It may involve fresh new connections, as in the celebrated work of Anne Sullivan with Helen Keller. It may involve a grouping and reordering of experiences to give them the kind of meaning the society gives them. It becomes richer and richer in meaning, especially in terms of value, that is, in terms of the affective quality which must be shared if the real, as seen by the group, is to be the real as seen by the child. The purely objective demonstration that things are different from the way the child assumes they are will only be a small part of the total task. There may be resistance organized in depth against giving up the precious fantasies of the early years, or there may be vested interests of many types organized around a role the child had given itself involving special power, prestige, lovableness, or importance.

The socialization of reality seeking is thus a matter of introducing levels of reality which are richer in value than those already existing in the individual. Since the whole definition of reality has arisen socially — and this means in many cases a conflict in values which underlies the conflict in the relative reality of ideas and ideals of contact — it will be only through social reconstruction of the real that the dominant factors in the child's thinking can be reached; the same is true, apparently, of the reality testing of adults. Something can be done by persuasion, something by objective demonstration of the way things are, something by reinforcement (that is, providing satisfying results for treating some things as real, and other things as unreal); but a great deal requires that emotional transformation which makes it safe and lovable to view things a certain way. This kind of reinforcement may have high dominance value and win the day.

MEDIATORS OF REALITY

We have been asserting all along that reality is *mediated* by specific agencies: sense organs, brain, striated and unstriated musculature, the body fluids, and countless inner agents. Clearly it is mediated before it ever makes its impact upon us, selected and channeled; in fact, the major task of human ecology is the study of the channels there are in the physical world antedating the cultural arrangements of mankind by which certain energies get through to us. Not only can we itemize piecemeal the various kinds of wave lengths that get through to us, as Herrick did in his *Introduction to Neurology,* thirty years ago, but we can, in the manner of Egon Brunswik, define the stimulus *textures,* the many sensory channels through which most things must pass with all their gating, facilitating, inhibiting processes, and the textures in the Gibsonian sense which act as cues for one or another type of reality. It is a mediated world that we encounter. It is not selected only in terms of attention. Attention is just the central and most obvious mediator between what we like to think of as inner and outer. The outer has its own system of hurdles and gating processes; so has the inner. In some respects they meet at the attending process.

The more formal training for the selection of relevant texture of the environment is that provided ordinarily by the mother, whose capacity to make real to the infant this or that, which he needs to know, is one of her primary motherhood roles. Then, as life gets a bit more complicated, there have to be mentors, teachers, or priests, with the general responsibility of transcending the role of the mother. Their roles relate to tribal, national, and common human realities, and also contain a capacity to implement and enforce — even to the point of painful puberty rites and initiation ceremonies — with the whole massive authority of the social group. The neighborhood and primary group have been supporting the mother, and now they are preparing for the official mentors of society at large. They seem, according to Eugene Lerner's data, to enforce the egocentrisms, the "sociocentrisms" of one community as against another.

We, the Reality Testers

But when we say it is the role of society to insist upon *this* real rather than *that* real — "orthodoxy is my doxy; heterodoxy is your doxy" — we encounter cross-cultural issues of a much more general sort. It is not only a question of *what* you believe and value. It is a question of how you value. It is a question of the atmospheres which are learned relating to social life at large and the learning process in particular. The discovery of reality is therefore group discovery. The story of the Curies, and Einstein's prediction that light would bend around a solid body, force not only the acceptance of new specific reals, but new *criteria* of reality. The whole issue today indeed as to what is to be believed regarding the credibility of the senses, the relation of brain to mind, the relation of morals to beauty, the relation of man's ideals to a cosmic pattern — all the issues touched upon briefly in this volume, and reaching out in all directions into a cosmos of soluble and insoluble problems for science and philosophy — have surely transcended the question of "what is real for me personally." In an age of science and technology, society determines the reorientation in philosophy and ethics, reconstitution of standards in the quest of reality. It is we, the reality testers, not I as an individual reality tester, that pose the insistent problems. The test of modern education is not whether it teaches to read, but whether it teaches something of the flavor of the predicament of modern man — twin questions relating to what he can expect to be able to know, and what he can expect by way of human relations across the globe. The realities of the next century, if there are some, will be realities discovered and implemented not by a man, but by mankind.

Yet the counterpart of this necessary accent upon the "common human" is implementation of social reality in terms of its implications for oneself. One does not seek alone, but in solitude one must apply what has been socially learned. From this viewpoint one learns one's place in the human group and in the cosmos, and defines as real that which meets the criteria of group life. One similarly develops an inner picture of self as a reality-seeking person because mankind with its new demand for reality will not allow any individual to slip through the mesh of the new net. Each individual will have to meet both a social criterion of the real, a definition of disciplined reality-testing procedures, and a conception of himself as one capable of sharing in all these endeavors.

Three conceptions of the self arise in this context. (1) The self that is perceived by the little child, mostly a physical self, together with sound of the voice, and in many instances, clothing and toys, etc., which give a core or central definition of selfhood. (2) A concept rather than a percept; a working idea of the self based upon what one can do, how one responds and is responded to by others, the functional or socially identifiable self. (3) The expanded or enlarged self, the self of object-relations, in which our early feeling-life is invested; the world of identification and identity; the world of membership in the social group. From this flows, in time, the tendency towards sharing other people's needs, seeing through their eyes, becoming — in some sense — identical with them in stance towards the world.

We raise these questions and semantic problems here because otherwise we might give the impression that we think of the physical self with its body boundaries, and the sharp separation of self from non-self, as the only self with which a theory of reality must come to terms. Actually the standards by which we are judging reality are often established and developed in terms of full social participation and group membership. That is real which is experienced by humans as they stand together against life's uncertainties; and at the third level, evaluation of what is meaningful depends to a considerable degree upon the investment in them, the coalescence of the narrow physical self-image, and the conceptual self, with the self as member of a larger social whole.

It is rather often forgotten that in the psychoanalytic system provision is made not only for intensely meaningful object-relationships, but for an identification process with others which mutes the sharpness of individual competition; also it is often forgotten that the superego, as defined by Freud, is only about half a matter of introjection of a disciplinary parent, the other half consists of an ego ideal which is, in fact, based upon affection and reciprocity between child and adult and remains — in a rich and stable personality — a profound counterpoise to the competitive self to which so many deprecatory terms are directed in the moralistics of today's social philosophy.

Dostoyevsky in *The Brothers Karamazov* has given us a vivid and moving portrayal of such affection and reciprocity between son and father in developing the relationship between Ilusha and Captain Snegiryov. In the following passage the father recounts his son's distress at having been witness to an unavenged insult to his father's honor.

"So in the evening I took the boy out for a walk, for you must know we go for a walk every evening, always the same way, along which we are going now — from our gate to that great stone which lies alone in the road under the hurdle, which marks the beginning of the town pasture. A beautiful and lonely spot, sir. Ilusha and I walked along hand in hand as usual. He has a little hand, his fingers are thin and cold — he suffers with his chest, you know. 'Father,' said he, 'father!' 'Well?' said I. I saw his eyes flashing. 'Father, how he treated you then!' 'It can't be helped, Ilusha,' I said. 'Don't forgive him, father, don't forgive him! At school they say that he has paid you ten roubles for it.' 'No, Ilusha,' said I, 'I would not take money from him for anything.' Then he began trembling all over, took my hand in both his and kissed it again. 'Father,' he said, 'father, challenge him to a duel, at school they say you are a coward and won't challenge him, and that you'll accept ten roubles from him.' 'I can't challenge him to a duel, Ilusha,' I answered. And I told briefly what I've just told you. He listened. 'Father,' he said, 'anyway don't forgive it. When I grow up I'll call him out myself and kill him.' His eyes shone and glowed. And of course I am his father, and I had to put in a word: 'It's a sin to kill,' I said, 'even in a duel.' 'Father,' he said, 'when I grow up, I'll knock him down, knock the sword out of his hand, I'll fall on him, wave my sword over him and say: "I could kill you, but I forgive you, so there!" You see what the workings of his little mind have been during these two days; he must have been planning that vengeance all day, and raving about it at night."

Life is not all friendliness, but neither is it all hostility. The ego is not all competition, and its reality testing is not all a function of what advances the individual in the struggle for a place in the sun.

In the same context it must be noticed that the executive ego, concerned with means as well as ends, is concerned with advancing group welfare, not personal welfare exclusively, and that the conception of reality testing in terms of meeting the mature judgments of the executive ego must therefore be redefined in terms of the area — specifically the social area — in which executive decisions are made. We support one another's judgments about reality not only because when in isolation we live, as Hobbes said, a life that is "dull, nasty, brutish, and short," but because by sharing a group-defined world we believe to be real, we let ourselves in not only for illusion, but for reality; not only for self-deception, but for social discovery.

13

The Immediate and the
Remote Environment

From the viewpoint developed here, one looks out towards
the near or far external environment, and looks in towards an
"internal environment," balancing between the tidal waves of
the two, yet managing somehow to mediate the outer to the
inner in terms of isomorphism, and at times finding in the
outer world what is at the very inmost heart of the self. The
"I," the observer, is not the inner, but stands paradoxically
between the inner and the outer.

There are additional good reasons why this should be true.
From the viewpoint of the studies of perception of outer and
inner worlds, many an inner event can be properly classified
by virtue of similarity to various outer events. What happens
within is of a piece with what is coming from without. Thus,
we experience warm and cool partly by virtue of the actual
warmth and coolness of liquids we take in, and also in terms
of the role of the capillaries in controlling a greater or smaller
amount of radiation, so that we are actually warm or cool
depending upon the environment; this means that we are

warm or cool in the skin and in the gastrointestinal system. By an easy metaphor, we are also warm to those we love and cool to those we dislike. There is, in other words, a primitive reality in our assuming the qualities of the outer world under those of the inner world, and vice versa.

This in turn begets a tendency to confuse the self with the outer world. It takes a while for the infantile "indissociation," as Piaget calls it, to evolve into a differentiated or structured world of outer and inner. The empirical self becomes slowly separated off, not only from the outer world of objects, but from the inner world of sensations from vital organs. The "self" is easily confused. At its edges, to speak metaphorically, much which is a part of myself, at this moment, will be peripheral to me an hour from now. Even the central core of self can be dissipated in panic or rage, to a point at which one does not know who one is. The "loss of ego boundaries" is a principle which applies not only to acts involving self-control, but even to the intimate awareness of selfhood. Through this line of evidence one may today approach the loss of self-awareness, which has been reported through the ages by mystics, by yoga adepts, by those brainwashed or overwhelmed by contradictory evidence regarding their identity. The term "depersonalization" may then be used both for feelings of strangeness, for experience of alienation, and for a genuine loss of awareness of individuality.

Cosmic Consciousness

One passes, therefore, into awareness of the cosmos in which one is not even a drop of independent existence, but is blended wholly with the cosmic reality. The frame of mind is usually "ecstatic." Occasionally it is unutterably terrible. For the most part, however, the bliss and the terror are somewhat predictable from the preceding attitudes, and there appear to be some states of loss of selfhood — perhaps the "break-off" states of the high altitude flier — in which this cognitive unification of self with world goes all the way to the loss of self-awareness without being particularly rich in affect. On historical grounds well justified by R. M. Bucke's selection and analysis of the experiences of the great mystics, and the copious reports available from modern users of psychedelic drugs, we may certainly say that ecstasy is characteristic of most such states. But the issue is confused because most of Bucke's cases and most of the modern psychedelic cases do not really involve a loss of self-awareness, only an enhancement of that joy which has been anticipated.

It would be intellectually easier and could possibly be in the right direction to suggest that the "loss" of self-awareness is seldom or never absolute, but that self has taken its model, its template perhaps, from cosmic structure and cosmic quality. Thus self, isomorphic with world, would resonate and become undifferentiated from the world. The little self, instead of setting itself up in the ordinary opposition to the outer world, blends in the symphony in which it becomes a tiny tone, ultimately to disappear into the cosmic symphony, with no awareness of its own individuality. Isomorphism could be pushed quite far as an explanatory principle, and it would appear to follow that competitive struggles for individuality or the demanding attitude towards the cosmos would interfere with cosmic consciouness of this type. If the "natural" state of man is one of relaxation, perhaps of a regressive restatement of an infantile balance with reference to the mother, or perhaps because of a complete fulfillment of self as one views the vast harmonies of the world, one might go on to say that the individual capacity for joy will determine the affective load such a state will carry. The joyous ones become supremely joyful; the affectively neutral merely become expanded perceivers of cosmic structure. The few who are riddled with inner fright will realize only terror in the new state.

We are not satisfied with this analysis, but at least the emphasis upon individuality will serve, in some measure, to set the stage for the affective as well as the cognitive. In fact, if what we have said about cognitive controls and affective style is sound, the person experiencing cosmic consciousness would not really be lost in the same world with all other experiencers of the same reality; rather, he would become more fully individuated, selecting from the cosmos what is deeply significant of himself. If this should be true, it would be quite different from the yoga conception of the loss of self in some completely impersonal cosmic scheme. Probably there is room for both ways of thinking — and perhaps of others.

How Remote Is the Remote?

We have had no great problem in bringing modern psychophysiological research into relation to the classical problems of philosophy about the knower and the known, and no great difficulty in assuming that new stance by which we look to the interior of the body as if it were an external object. However, we now encounter a very large new challenge. We are looking for a kind of environment which is more "distal" than the distal kind of environment which, though cosmic and though our source and origin racially and individually, we have regarded as beyond our ken. Only today we are finding that it is not beyond our ken at all, but capable of being touched; in fact, it is being touched in a wide variety of ways. We are discovering electromagnetic waves like cosmic rays which not only pass through us, but at times collide with something inside us, and cause disease or, in some cases, act as a source of restoration. We find that this cosmic environment actually occasions new directions in evolution, as the impact of cosmic rays causes mutations; not only are the germ cells encountered by packaged energies from a remote corner of the universe, but these energies set going new lethal, and sometimes constructive, possibilities within human or subhuman genes.

These are but a few examples of the tremendous impact the cosmic environment is known to have upon many by channels only recently discovered, and on a scale altogether staggering. Cosmic rays were for a while belittled; but they are now beginning to be understood as merely the first known representatives of a tremendous line of energies, some observable by modern instrumentation today, some waiting for tomorrow. The rapid discovery of more and more types of electrical particles and more and more wave forms make it very improbable that we have seen the last of these new cosmic messages. Indeed, we have probably only begun the story. Moreover, these strange messages travel in media we have scarcely begun to recognize at all. Three-quarters of a century ago, the onslaught began on the conception of the ether. Consideration of a series of events, passing through the minds of Planck and Einstein, de Broglie, Bohr, and Heisenberg, have established the probability of a field system of energy far more subtle than those of the simple electromagnetism of a few decades past. In fact, we now face the very high probability that there are a great variety of events which are indirectly projected into the world modern science can know. But the science of day-after-tomorrow will deal more directly with these hidden sources of today's manifestations.

Let us allow ourselves this analogy. In looking down a microscope one typically sees tiny particles moving to and fro as if bombarded by an invisible agent. This is the Brownian movement. It looks like a bombardment because it is a bombardment. Large molecules, which have an appreciable momentum relative to the object, keep the visible particles under bombardment moving this way and that as long as we care to watch. There is a sub-visible world, so to speak, which is the cause of changes in the visible world. Now this is exactly the view to which we appear to be driven today, with regard to events which are detectable by delicate modern physical equipment, but the sources of which are unobservable. Dr. Francis Bitter of the Massachusetts Institute of Technology writes: "We are more and more certain that in empty space, devoid of atoms, there is an even more complex activity. There are many, many overlapping fields which pass mass and energy to and fro, which have symmetry and design, which affect our lives."

It is probable, in fact, that our sense organs constantly respond to these invisible agents, and likewise that our brains also do so. The cosmic rays are relatively crude and obvious today, compared with a great many energy relations existing and starting to creep in upon us. The possibility is always open that what all those around us regard as unreal is that to which *we*, at the moment, are responding in a definite, though as yet undemonstrable, fashion. If there is something in us which lies hidden there in cosmic structure, we may indeed apprehend it in an extrasensory fashion.

Cosmic Consciousness and Joy

Against this background we may consider some of the possible meanings of peak experiences or of cosmic consciousness. The first and most obvious consideration is that thresholds may momentarily be lowered so that energies or impacts ordinarily shut out may be received.

The second possibility is that the channels may be open at the time because there is no competition from alternative requirements for their use — no competition, for example, from ego preoccupations such as competition for immediate self-enhancement. We might call this an "ego fadeout."

This raises in a new form the question of why such experiences are ordinarily joyful. It would be easy to answer that this is because joy is the natural state of man, and that we need only to remove competition or egoism which is the primary source of distress. But this would not cover the fact that some joyful mystical experiences are ego-fulfillment states rather than ego-abrogation states.

We think there is a simpler explanation. It starts from an evolutionary premise. The very first thing an organism has to do is to continue to exist; then it must grow, repair itself, reproduce itself. These are intrinsically self-fulfilling. From an evolutionary point of view, organisms which are fulfilled in a deep sense in carrying out these activities are well attuned to their environment, and likely to be able to live; so are the species, varieties, and individual strains which make a go of life requirements. Pleasure, happiness, joy, or whatever it is called, is not a sign of the devil's claw, but when analyzed through its roots, an indication that tissues are doing what they came into existence to do. From this viewpoint the pleasure centers in the brain are vigorously excited when effective adaptation is achieved. The real should be a joyful thing.

There will be complications and we shall try to face them. There seems to be no mystery about the fact that self-realization in the philosophical sense is a source both of triumph and of delight. From this point of view, the presence of the ego does not alter the basic logic at all. It merely means that at times, if the ego is really integrated, it may occasion experiences of joy; whereas, if it is disintegrated through setting up sources of frustration, it may sap the vitality of the organism and lower the pleasure level.

Cosmic Consciousness and Individuality

But these same states of enhancement should increase the readiness for the reception of cosmic energies into and with them. There is fresh resonance. The discovery of appropriate "wave lengths," as in the case of photic driving, is effected; there is greater openness to cosmic messages in general insofar as there is attunement to them. Whether there is such a thing as attunement to all wave lengths, a sort of pan-sensitization, a sort of tuning which would allow all wave lengths (compare "white noise" and all tonal components in a tumultuous and crashing atonal impact) is hard to believe. Tuning would be selective even if there were hundreds of tones to be brought into the receiver; one may be sure that no two would ever draw upon the same combination of rhythms. It might well be that a person could exist here and there who is in tune with everything, or as a cliché has it, "in tune with the infinite," but it would seem more likely that what is meant is attunement to a rich variety of concordant forms of stimulation, a capacity to draw from the spectrum of reality a very large number of mutually compatible hues. One person's "cosmic consciousness" could be like that of another either through the sharing of a large number of essential components, or through a feeling tone which is the same for different combinations — as, for example, in the works of Mozart, passages may feel alike, though in tone, orchestration, and rhythm, the musicologist may call them very different. Individual differences here may be a matter of cognitive style.

WHAT IS THERE?

Now if the rhythm within the central nervous system is actually the rhythm of the distant stimulating agency, there is a sense in which one apprehends the distant energy source, whether one is in sensory contact with it or not. The important thing is that the mathematical form of the wave be the same. As E. B. Holt pointed out in his essay in *The New Realism*, to make contact or even identity out of our relation to a thing known is a form of realism. To contact with a universal was Plato's realism. To make contact with the mind of God was Berkeley's realism. To make contact with the wave form of a cosmic energy is Holt's kind of realism.

Bertrand Russell, skirting this problem, made a characteristically brilliant observation which we think marks a hair's breadth "near miss," and in an instance in which "a miss is as good as a mile." In his celebrated essay, "A Free Man's Worship," he undertook to insist that there is nothing in the universe which has any sympathy or concern or even correspondence with what is at the heart of man. He argued that man cannot reach out to the cosmos. Man can only isolate or encyst himself from it, and set up within this little encysted pocket a world where human warmth, esthetic and ethical values can subsist.

We would take exception to Russell's view on two grounds. As one surveys the tooth and claw of evolutionary sequence and the wars, genocides, and daily brutalities of humankind, one is forced to conclude that this little pocket of human life established by Russell in "The Free Man's Worship" has to include all that is known to be human; it must include the violent as well as the gentle, the chaotic as well as the ordered, disciplined, and thoughtful. It is in *humanity*, or life in an inclusive sense that the principle of "The Free Man's Worship" can find its basis.

But beyond this and in light of the position we have been

developing, we raise the question why the principles of rationality and affection, alongside of violence and chaos, ever got established at all, to achieve such places as they now have in the evolutionary schema and a status as values that make some sort of appeal to reflective mankind. It is perhaps not demonstrable at this time, but we suggest that these principles, too, are immanent in cosmic structure and that their resonance reaches out to something in man. The question of how far these particular resonant components can be developed within us and how much they will find in the universe with which they can make contact is a question towards which the present volume attempts a groping answer.

For certainly it cannot be claimed that human nature is in perfect resonance with some sort of a perfect cosmos. There is certainly a problem of selection. Indeed, even in the highest peak experiences it does not appear, from the record, that one makes total contact. There is a high degree of selectivity. We certainly cannot reject fractional contact or fragmentary cathexis. They may, at times, be fatal to integration because one may stop, as in the Freudian fixation, incapable of moving onwards. But there is always an editing process to be done, and no less so in the case of the editing of the presented reality, for the sake of some sort of meaningful integration. Flooding here is to be feared, as in all kinds of overload, in all kinds of sensory enrichment. The experience of the investigators of psychedelic drugs, like that of yoga and mysticism generally, constantly reminds us that selectivity, order, discipline — in short, "form" — must be maintained, or there is nothing.

Cosmic Consciousness and Parapsychology

This is not a book about parapsychology, or a considerable discussion would be needed here of the fact that these contacts by means other than the usual channels of the senses, are of course among primary problems whose solution lies apparently along the same paths we have been treading. Instead of making contact, however, with very distant time-space realities, as in mystical experiences, contacts are made with not very distant, not very far removed in time, events in the lives of other persons; the following is a typical "spontaneous telepathic case," reported in letter form:

Brantwood, Coniston
October 27th, 1883

I woke up with a start, feeling I had had a hard blow on my mouth, and with a distinct sense that I had been cut, and was bleeding under my lip, and seized my pocket-handkerchief, and held it (in a little pushed lump) to the part, as I sat up in bed, and after a few seconds, when I removed it, I was astonished not to see any blood, and only then realized it was impossible anything could have struck me there, as I lay fast asleep in bed, and so I thought it was only a dream! — but I looked at my watch, and saw it was seven, and finding Arthur (my husband) was not in the room, I concluded (rightly) that he must have gone out on the lake for an early sail, as it was so fine.

I then fell asleep. At breakfast (half-past nine), Arthur came in rather late, and I noticed he rather purposely sat farther away from me than usual, and every now and then put his pocket-handkerchief furtively up to his lip, in the very way I had done. I said, 'Arthur, why are you doing that?' and added a little anxiously, 'I know you've hurt yourself! But I'll tell you why afterwards.' He said, 'Well, when I was sailing, a sudden squall came, throwing the tiller suddenly round, and it struck me a bad blow in the mouth, under the upper lip, and it has been bleeding a good deal and won't stop.' I then said, 'Have you any idea what o'clock it was when it happened?' and he answered, 'It must have been about seven.'

I then told what had happened to *me*, much to *his* surprise, and all who were with us at breakfast.

It happened here about three years ago at Brantwood, to me.

Joan R. Severn.

Taking into account the notion of contact with distant events, as in telepathy experiments over huge distances, now running to some several dozen investigations, there are also the cases of sudden presentation of the past or the future as if it were a part of the living now. Referring back to the cases of *déjà vu* and the shift in time position cited there, there are a good many well recorded cases in which the person somehow makes contact directly with an event in some other person's past, or an event in the past of the cosmic process itself.

The following is a portion of a case report, based on a detailed investigation by the senior author and a psychiatrist, Herbert L. Klemme, which upon completion strongly suggested an authentic occurrence of retrocognition:

On October 3, 1963, Mrs. Coleen Buterbaugh, secretary to Dean Sam Dahl, of Nebraska Wesleyan University, Lincoln, Nebraska, was asked by Dean Dahl to take a message to a colleague, Professor Martin (pseudonym), in his office suite in the C. C. White Building nearby. At about 8:50 A.M. Mrs. Buterbaugh entered this building and walked briskly along its extensive hall, hearing the sounds of students in a group of rooms set aside for music practice, and notably a marimba playing. Entering the first room of the suite, she took about four steps and was stopped short by a very intense odor — a musty, disagreeable odor. Raising her eyes, she saw the figure of a very tall, black-haired woman in a shirtwaist and ankle-length skirt who was extending her right arm to the upper righthand shelves in an old music cabinet. We now continue the account in Mrs. Buterbaugh's own words:

. . . As I first walked into the room everything was quite normal. About four steps into the room was when the strong odor hit me. When I say strong odor, I mean the kind that simply stops you in your track and almost chokes you. I was looking down at the floor, as one often does when walking, and as soon as that odor stopped me I felt that there was someone in the room with me. It was then that I was aware that there were no noises out in the hall. Everything was deathly quiet. I looked up and something drew my eyes to the cabinet along the wall in the next room. I looked up and there she was. She had her back to me, reaching up into one of the shelves of the cabinet with her right hand, and standing perfectly still. She wasn't at all aware of my presence. While I was watching her she never moved. She was not transparent and yet I knew she wasn't real. While I was looking at her she just faded away — not parts of her body one at a time, but her whole body all at once.

Up until the time she faded away I was not aware of anyone else being in the suite of rooms, but just about the time of her fading out I felt as though I still was not alone. To my left was a desk and I had a feeling there was a man sitting at that desk. I turned around and saw no one, but I still felt his presence. When that feeling of his presence left I have no idea, because it was then, when I looked out the window behind that desk, that I got frightened and left the room. I am not sure whether I ran or walked out of the room. Doctor Murphy, when I looked out that window there wasn't one modern thing out there. The street (Madison Street), which is less than a half-block away from the building, was not even there and neither was the new Willard House. That was when I *realized that these people were not in my time, but that I was back in their time.*

The thesis suggested here is that "contact" with the distant in space and with the distant in time, whether past or future, is functionally similar to the basic perceptual responses which go on all the time, utilizing energies now better understood in terms of their impacts upon sense organs. There is very limited understanding of the kinds of impact made directly by cosmic energies upon the central nervous system itself, and there is practically no understanding at all of the energies which may impinge upon us through that sub-molecular world mentioned above. It is likely, however, that all of these types of impacts have something in common, for they are all manifest in the same universe and are all expressions of the same ultimate architectural expression in time and space.

14

What Kinds of Reality Are Sought?

We find ourselves at length in a strange concordance with Immanuel Kant and, at the same time, with a strange alienation from his modality of thought. With the struggle to make sense, as well as he could, out of Hume's skepticism, and in an effort to utilize the new astronomy and physics of the eighteenth century, he laid down some of the fundamental laws of thought relating to what can ever be known, judged, concluded. As he compared the "dogmatic slumbers" from his earliest years with the profound doubts of David Hume, he came to the conclusion that we can only know in terms of a finite, limited human group of intellectual capacities. We have to experience things in terms of space and time and cannot hope to know the reality mediated by our time and space experiences. We cannot hope to know what is really out there, the noumena, the things in themselves beyond our apprehending minds, from which knowledge proceeds.

Kant is naturally regarded by one large wing of modern philosophy as the first great prophet who really understood the limitations of man's claim upon knowledge, and the claim upon the reality with which knowledge tries to deal. On the other hand, he has been rejected as an archenemy who destroyed confidence in rationality. He made it necessary to look to faith to discover the realities by which man must live: God, freedom, and immortality. The nineteenth century went ahead with its scientific discoveries in the physical, biological, and social sciences, bowing to Kant here and there, and certainly profoundly acknowledging his conception that it is only that which is formulated mathematically that we can confidently accept as known. On the whole, however, science created a mass of independent data by cross-confirmation from different sense organs, just as Aristotle asked, by cross-confirmation of perceptual evidence from rational evidence (as in the case of the physics of Planck and Einstein), and by resolutely pursuing the matter of man's own relativity and of the relativity of social viewpoints as we have faced these problems above. The result has not actually been reinstatement of Kant. It has not at all suggested the absolute rejection of absolute knowledge in the form Kant thought he had vindicated. One has come today to the conception that, although no one method of knowledge can yield absolute knowledge, there is a mutual compatibility, a mutual reinforcement of various types of perceptual and rational evidence. From the stance achieved by utilizing many approaches to knowledge, one may look out upon the universe with a considerably greater degree of confidence, through cross-checking, that there is something in the total system which "corresponds" in some way to a reality as man construes it. It is true that the "correspondence theory of truth" is itself still open to argument, but some sort of correspondence works as well in the tough realities of living as in dealing with engineering and medical problems, and the conception of the unknowability of the universe has tended to recede.

ISOMORPHISM AND REALITY

It is especially the conception of isomorphism, of which we have made so much, which strongly supports the view that one does apprehend realities because they are the very stuff of which one's own immediate self-awareness is made. One may, if one likes, deny that this is reality, but one wonders if the term "real" would still, on that basis, have a meaning. In setting up as real that which is immediately apprehended — and not claiming for it any meanings which are not apprehended, merely because they are "logical" — there is the large likelihood that we may systematize these various types of apprehension both within ourselves and from one person to another, and may develop a reasonably congruent and workable reality, social as well as personal, and cosmic as well as social. Kant is left with a perfectly legitimate glory in having established the problems absolutism and relativity would have to face, but he is apparently not left with any certain vindication in his denial that reality, both outer and inner, can be apprehended. It is through the knower's isomorphism of inner and outer aspects placed on either side of the knowing process that the problem of reality seems to be in the process of being solved.

An evolutionary approach, even before Darwin, showed that there was a new way to restate Kant's position. We could say not that man is stuck forever with a hopeless incapacity to know, but rather that his evolutionary development predisposes him to select, organize, know, and interpret in certain ways rather than others. This, as we saw, was the process lying behind pragmatism. It was plainly the basis for William James' conception of "necessary truths," the truths which spring from our relation to the natural order in which we must live, and to which we must assign meaning. More recently it is the basis for a theory of cognition in which physical realities and psychological realities are brought closer together. Here the Gestalt psychologists and the psychoanalysts make their own contributions to the theory of knowledge; here Piaget's "genetic epistemology" comes to grips with the more formal logic and mathematics of the Newtonian era. One may seek the true, pure logic of an unfolding mind confronting in the schoolroom the realities of modern mathematics, but one must in turn understand the living system in which ideas of this sort germinate and grow.

We have found a good deal in human nature which can be said to seek reality, to search, scan, attain, and funnel in the various aspects of the outer milieu and of the inner milieu as well. As we move towards a conclusion, the question may appear to arise: is it "real reality" that we want? Is there a basic universal human craving to make contact with reality?

We have found many points where there are shortcuts leading in some such direction as this, and implying an affirmative answer. We have found much evidence of the adequacy of sense organs and central nervous system to grasp, rearrange, and act upon messages in such fashion as to make a real contact with a real world. We have, nevertheless, found the process to be highly selective at all phases, from the outer foundations of the universe through to the ultra-microscopic electronic details of the human interior. We have found no evidence that the *whole pattern* of truth or reality, if there is such a thing, is actively sought; in fact, we have found that chaos would lie along that road. We have, then, made our basic question more selective. Instead of asking whether man seeks reality, we have asked what kinds of reality are *capable* of being *defined,* and among these, which kinds are *capable* of being *pursued,* and within this final category, which kinds are *actually* pursued.

Our first reply is that there is no formal quest of reality as such. Insofar as worlds of varying degrees of reality can be defined as one grows in a social milieu, one may strive for one rather than another kind of reality.

Moreover, in the isomorphic response, the affirmative answer is sometimes given us by definition, or at least by definition and extrapolation. As Tannegay de Quénetain shows, the order of the psychophysiological response to the rhythms and tonalities of music may be the order of the orchestral production itself. The body may receive and maintain the essential structure which is there in the stimulus configuration, and the music is "sublime" or just "trivial" depending upon the degree to which this order is maintained. We have already seen reason to doubt that this is a purely arbitrary socio-cultural product. The bodily rhythms, the symmetries, the ups and downs of sine wave form, the mathematics of integrated tonality in the composer's imagination take their cue from realities that are there in the very nature of sound, there in the nature of our physiology, and there in the nature of our psychological response.[1]

When the creative artist seeks a solution, he seeks a real, not an unreal. He seeks a kind of order which is implicit in the material, and a kind of order which even a modern computer can extract from the complexities of tone, just as an averaging instrument may toss out various kinds of "noise," and lay bare the structural beauty and order of a complex system of tones in ordered temporal relations. The Greeks had the same conception regarding sculpture and architecture; much of it, as we know, was derived from the Pythagorean school of southern Italy, and much of it came through Plato into the general numerological system preserved to this day as a clue to reality. Galileo carried this forward from Pythagoras and Plato to the mathematics of Newton and modern science. There is no longer any reasonable place for a purely subjective definition of man's conception of the beautiful and the good insofar as these can be demonstrated to be deeply built into his evolutionary, genetic, developmental sequence, and into the sociocultural principles which embody, in large social outlines, what is necessary for man as man. Flexibility and relativity are indeed part of the very nature of man.

[1] It is relevant here to draw a distinction between our conception of the isomorphic relationship between the known and the knowable and Alfred North Whitehead's view of "organism" as the fundamental universal "event." For us, isomorphism implies an identity of structural principles in the organic and inorganic spheres, in cosmos and organism. Consciousness is an interface or a mirror in which these principles are reflected in the form of percepts, concepts, and values. In Whitehead's view, what man experiences as cognitive and valuational activity is ingredient in the event-constituted structure of the universe and at every level of organization from sub-atomic inorganic to molecular organic. Thus while for us in this book, isomorphism is a principle that may be seen as relating organism and cosmos, for Whitehead the fundamental building block of his cosmology, the *event*, is *organism* with perceiving, cognizing, and valuing attributes.

However, order, and a fairly limited order, for man as a species, is likewise there. Consequently, to the question: "Is it 'real reality' that we want?" the answer is *sometimes* clearly "yes."

But the answer has implied the recognition of levels of reality. From a strictly Aristotelian point of view, the statement is true or false, and a portrayed situation may be real or not real. From the point of view developed at the beginning of this volume, expectations may be fulfilled or frustrated. The whole drift of our analysis, however, has suggested that there are degrees of biological readiness for events; degrees of consistency and confidence in the formulation of what is, and also what is to be; degrees of coherence in the various measures taken by the individual to confront the various uncertain aspects of the immediate future; degrees of reality in the symbolic representation of the world. There is, consequently, a place for things which are more real and less real. There are memories, as we saw, which are "too real." There are experiences of self and relation to world which are "not real enough." There are scientific observations which bring the real intensely, vitally, excitingly near. There are types of yogic exercises which enhance the sense of reality. There are psychedelic drugs which make real more real than it ever was before.

The task of living is one of defining for oneself, within a sociocultural norm, a conception of what can be expected, a conception of how far it can be modified, a conception of how it can be transfigured by creative imagination. Reality is being perpetually edited. It is this editing of the real, this calling into existence of that which was only potentially there, and of turning back again into the potential that which a minute ago was real, that is the process of facing the real and of creating the real.

From the present viewpoint there is always more. There is more stuff. There are more processes. There are more systems. There are more legitimate forms of conceptualization and abstraction as we discover more and more. The endless seeking, searching, scanning processes increase both the range and the depth of the real, both the number and variety of real things, and the levels of structure which the architecture of the universe may allow us to observe, until we strive to observe even the apex of the pyramid, the top architectural plan of the real as a whole. It is profoundly satisfying and self-enhancing to do this, and this may be one of the things which make the cosmic experiences more joyous. If this should involve both the increasing range or extensity of the things and processes that are swept within our ken, and at the same time a deepening understanding of the problem of reality itself, we can literally say that there is progress towards the real.

Glossary

Adaptation level: The stimuli in a series which evoke a neutral response; the subjective centroid of a stimulus series about which perceptual judgments are ordered

Apperceptive mass: The already existing knowledge with which the apprehended qualities of an object are articulated or related in such a way as to be understood

Autism: In general, cognitive functioning in which needs, wishes, or affects determine the result more than does reality

Autonomic nervous system: The part of the nervous system which supplies the vital organs and smooth musculature with their efferent innervation

Canalization: Progressive shift in differential response to the various means of satisfying a drive

Cathexis: Degree of affective significance or "energy value" of an object, person, or idea

Cognition: Any process by means of which one arrives at knowledge

Conditioning, classical: Often referred to as "Pavlovian Conditioning." It is a learning procedure in which a neutral stimulus (called a conditioned stimulus, CS) comes to elicit a response (called a conditioned response, CR) which resembles the response (unconditioned response, UR) normally given to another stimulus (unconditioned stimulus, US)

Conditioning, operant: A learning procedure in which the experimenter alters the strength of an emitted response by reinforcing it whenever it is emitted

Core-context theory: A theory of perceptual meaning espoused by E. B. Titchener which states that at any moment there is a core of stimulations or percepts, to which we are attending, which are given meaning by their context of contiguous stimulations, images, or ideas

Depersonalization: A state in which a person loses the feeling of his own reality or feels his body to be unreal

Ego: According to Freud, an aspect of the personality which is in contact with the external world by means of perception, thought, and reality-regulated striving

Epicritic sensibility: Cutaneous sensing of light touch, warmth, coolness, and delicate localization

Epistemology: The philosophical study of the origin, nature, and limits of knowledge

Exteroceptor: A sense organ stimulated directly by energy changes outside the body

Extrasensory perception: A response to an external event not presented to any known sense

Feedback: The signals in a system which return (are fed back) to the input. If these signals oppose or inhibit the input, they are called *negative feedback*. If they facilitate or amplify the input, they are called *positive feedback*

Function: The activity proper to or distinctive of a structure

Gestalt: (a) Literally translated from the German as "*form*." (b) An organized pattern or configuration. (c) A system of psychology which emphasizes (b).

Homeostasis: The tendency to maintain a stable system

Id: According to Freud, that division of the psyche from which come blind, impersonal, instinctual impulses

Imprinting: The one-trial or extremely rapid conditioning of certain behavior at critical stages of maturation when these behaviors occur in the presence of releasing stimuli

Inhibition: The stopping or restraining of a process from starting or continuing

Interoceptor: A sense organ or receptor inside the body in contrast with one near or at the surface

Metaphysics: A branch of philosophy concerned with the ultimate nature of existence

Parapsychology: A division of psychology dealing with psychological phenomena that appear not to fall within the range of what is presently covered by natural law

Perception: Interpretation of a stimulus

Pragmatism: The philosophical doctrine that the meaning of anything derives from its practical consequences

Proprioceptor: Any receptor sensitive to the position and movement of the body and its members

Protopathic sensibility: Cutaneous sensing in which only gross discrimination or localization is manifest

Psychosomatic: Having reference to disorders in which physiological symptoms are thought to have psychogenic origin

Scotoma: In vision, a blind spot. Metaphorically, a "mental blind spot" or area in which one cannot appreciate anything that conflicts with the egoistic pattern

Smooth muscle: A muscle presenting a smooth appearance under the microscope and involved chiefly in promoting internal adjustment

Solipsism: A philisophical view that one can be certain of nothing but one's own experience

Stimulation: (a) Reception of a stimulus. (b) The form of energy which a stimulus takes on when it is received and transformed

Striped muscle: A muscle bearing a striped appearance under the microscope. Usually attached to the skeleton and involved in movement of the organism in the environment

Structure: Any enduring arrangement, grouping, pattern, or articulation of parts to form a relatively stable system or whole

Threshold-Limen: (a) Absolute threshold: limit of size, intensity, position, etc., at which a stimulus becomes effective for conscious processes or behavior or ceases to be effective. (b) Difference threshold: smallest difference between two stimuli which can be discriminated

References

The method of documentation aims to keep the text as free as possible from footnotes, and to avoid reference numbers in the text. In most cases the name of the investigator in the text permits immediate use of the Bibliography. However, if the Bibliography lists several pieces of research by one investigator (or if, as happens here and there, research findings are noted in passing without mention of the investigator's name in the text), the following procedure is used:

Reference is given by page, paragraph, and line. The number following each proper name is the number of the item in the Bibliography. The reference is usually "anchored" on the name of the investigator mentioned in the text. When no name is cited, a salient part of the sentence is used as anchor. Paragraph 1 indicates the opening lines on a page, even when these are the continuation of a paragraph beginning on a preceding page.

13	1	4	Freud, S. (28)
14	2	1	Darwin, C. (19)
	2	18	Simpson, G. G. (102)
	3	12	Sokolov, N. Ye. (106)
15	1	7	Helson, H. (40)
	2	6	Yensen, R. (123)
	3	1	Pfaffman, C. (88)
	3	4	Klein, G. S. (60)
	3	8	Freud, S. (30)
	3	9	Rosenzweig, S. (96)

16	3	4	Smock, C. D., & Holt, B. G. (104)
17	1	1	Moore, H. T. (79)
	3	6	Woodworth, R. S. (122)
	3	10	Bühler, K. (13)
18	2	2	Polyak, S., & Willner, E. N. (91)
	2	12	Penfield, W. (87)
19	2	16	Sokolov, N. Ye (106)
20	1	20	Pfaffman, C. (88)

142

21 1 2 Holt, E. B. (46)
   1 6 Helmholtz, H. L. F. (39)
   4 4 Delgado, J. M. R. (21)
21 4 5 Olds, J., & Milner, P. (82)
24 3 5 Holt, E. B. (46)
25 1 9 Freud, S. (29)
   1 13 Gesell, A., & Amatruda, C. (32)
26 1 8 Craig, W. (18)
   3 2 Lorenz, K. (69)
27 2 1 Hess, E. H. (44)
   3 1 Scott, J. P. (99)
   3 5 Harlow, H. F. (35)
   4 8 Lund, F. H. (70)
28 2 1 Piaget, J. (89)
   2 7 Sokolov, N. Ye. (106)
   2 8 Helson, H. (40)
29 2 4 Kant, I. (58)
31 1 1 Hartley, D. (36)
   2 2 Spence, K. W. (108)
   3 2 Condillac, E. (16)
   4 2 Herbart, J. F. (41)
32 3 2 Uexküll, J. J. (115)
   5 4 Koffka, K. (62)
   5 5 Stern, W. (110)
33 2 2 Stern, W. (110)
   2 5 McNamara, H. J., & Fisch, R. I. (77)
   3 4 Piaget, J. (90)
34 1 4 Sherrington, C. (101)
35 1 2 Sherrington, C. (101)
   2 2 Gibson, J. J. (34)
   2 3 Gibson, E. J., & Walk, R. D. (33)

   2 12 Spitz, R. A. (109)
   3 7 Holzman, P. S., *et al.*, (48)
   3 10 Spence, D. P., & Holland, B. (107)
37 2 5 Murray, H. A. (81)
40 2 2 Pavlov, I. P. (85)
   2 5 Anokhin, P. K. (1)
   3 1 Zener, K. (124)
41 3 2 Pavlov, I. P. (85)
   3 8 Thorndike, E. L. (113)
42 3 3 Pavlov, I. P. (85)
   3 5 Razran, G. (93, 94)
43 1 2 Pavlov, I. P. (85)
   2 1 Razran, G. (93, 94)
   4 1 Whorf, B. L. (17)
44 1 9 Osgood, C. E. (84)
   3 1 Hernández-Peón, R., *et al.*, (42)
   3 13 Titchener, E. (114)
46 3 6 Titchener, E. (114)
47 1 10 Krech, D., *et al.*, (64)
   1 16 Brunswik, E. (11)
48 1 1 Sherrington, C. (101)
   2 9 Hebb, D. (37)
   2 13 Krech, D., *et al.*, (64)
49 3 2 Hebb, D. (37)
   3 3 Wiesel, T. N., & Hubel, D. H. (121)
50 1 4 Eddington, A. (23)
   2 2 Bernard, C. (6)
51 2 1 Bleuler, E. (8)
52 2 6 Rapaport, D. (92)
   3 2 Voth, H., & Mayman, M. (117)

53	1	7	Rapaport, D. (92)
54	3	7	Rapaport, D. (92)
	3	13	Freud, S. (30)
	4	3	Frenkel-Brunswik, E. (26)
56	2	2	Bykov, K. M. (14)
	2	7	Makarov, P. O. (73)
57	1	9	Hull, C. (49)
	2	5	Janet, P. (55)
59	1	6	Kleitman, N. (61)
60	1	6	James, W. (52)
61	1	3	Jung, C. G. (56)
	1	5	Voth, H., & Mayman, M. (117)
	2	8	Rapaport, D. (92)
62	1	5	Wiener, N. (120)
	2	5	Smith, K. U., *et al.*, (103)
	4	1	Holzman, P. S., & Rousey, C. (47)
64	2	1	Braatoy, T. (9)
	2	7	Reich, W., (95)
	3	3	Jacobson, E. (51)
	3	3	Max, L. W. (75)
65	1	3	Hefferline, R. F., *et al.*, (38)
	2	1	Davidowitz, J. (20)
	3	7	Lisina, M. I. (68)
66	1	11	Lisina, M. I. (68)
	1	14	Brener, J., & Hothersall, D. (10)
	1	14	Hnatiow, M., & Lang, P. J. (45)
	2	16	Rapaport, D. (92)
	2	18	Kamiya, J. (57)
70	2	1	Pavlov, I. P. (85)
	2	2	Bekhterev, V. M. (4)
	2	10	Malmo, R. B. (71)
71	2	3	Wenger, M. A., *et al.*, (118)
	2	16	Lisina, M. I. (68)
72	3	5	Penfield, W. (86)
73	4	3	Penfield, W. (87)
74	2	14	James, W. (53)
	3	6	Kohler, I. (63)
	3	6	Snyder, F. W., & Pronko, N. H. (105)
75	2	17	Smith, K. U., *et al.*, (103)
76	1	5	Orwell, G. (83)
79	2	1	Mannheim, K. (72)
80	2	5	Kilpatrick, F. P. (59)
81	2	26	McNamara, H. J. (76)
	2	29	Kilpatrick, F. P. (59)
83	1	1	Kilpatrick, F. P. (59)
86	1	1	Hernández-Peón, R., *et al.*, (42)
	1	4	Braatoy, T. (9)
87	1	1	Freud, S. (28)
	3	9	Freud, A. (27)
88	3	4	James, W. (53)
	3	5	Masefield, J. (74)
89	1	6	Ashby, W. R. (2)
90	1	6	Santos, J. F., *et al.*, (98)
91	1	8	McNamara, H. J., & Fisch, R. I. (77)
92	3	1	Helson, H. (40)
	3	1	Piaget, J. (89)
93	1	4	Piaget, J. (89)
	1	22	Herbart, J. F. (41)
96	1	8	James, W. (54)
	1	11	Laski, M. (65)
	1	13	Taylor, B. (112)

97 1 1 Meyer, E., & Covi,
         L. (78)
98 2 3 Herbart, J. F. (41)
101 2 2 Lecky, P. (66)
102 2 1 Lecky, P. (66)
     2 2 Erikson, E. H. (24)
     2 10 Freud, S. (29)
     3 10 Frank, L. K. (25)
     3 12 Useem, J. (116)
104 2 2 Camus, A. (15)
105 1 9 Janet, P. (55)
     2 4 Gardner, R., *et al.*,
         (31)
     2 4 Klein, G. S. (60)
106 1 18 Rapaport, D. (92)
110 1 7 Sokolov, N. Ye.
         (106)
     2 5 James, W. (54)
     3 1 Berlyne, D. E. (5)
     3 4 Sherrington, C.
         (101)
115 2 10 Herrick, J. C. (43)
     2 12 Brunswick, E. (11)
     2 15 Gibson, J. J. (34)
116 1 6 Lerner, E. (67)

     2 5 Bateson, G. (3)
118 2 5 Freud, S. (28)
     3 1 Dostoyevsky, F.
         (22)
121 2 3 Piaget, J. (89)
122 1 1 Bucke, R. M. (12)
124 2 13 Bitter, F. (7)
127 2 6 Holt, E. B. (46)
     3 1 Russell, B. (97)
129 2 1 Severn, J. (100)
130 2 2 Murphy, G., &
         Klemme, H. L.
         (80)
132 1 2 Kant, I. (58)
     1 4 Hume, D. (50)
133 1 7 Kant, I. (58)
134 1 12 Kant, I. (58)
     2 1 Darwin, C. (19)
     2 8 James, W. (53)
     2 15 Piaget, J. (89)
135 5 3 Tannegay de
         Quénetain (111)
136 3 3 Whitehead, A. N.
         (119)

Bibliography

1. ANOKHIN, P. K. The role of the orienting exploratory reaction in the formation of the conditioned reflex. In L. G. Voronin, et al. (Eds.), *Orienting reflex and exploratory behavior*. Baltimore: American Institute of Biological Sciences, 1965, 3–16.

2. ASHBY, W. R. *Design for a brain*. New York: Wiley, 1952.

3. BATESON, G. Social planning and the concept of "deutero-learning." In *Conference on science, philosophy and religion, second symposium*. New York: Harper, 1942.

4. BEHKTEREV, V. M. *General principles of human reflexology*. New York: International, 1932.

5. BERLYNE, D. E. *Conflict, arousal and curiosity*. New York: McGraw-Hill, 1960.

6. BERNARD, C. *An introduction to the study of experimental medicine*. (Transl., H. C. Green). New York: Dover, 1957.

7. BITTER, F. *Magnets, the education of a physicist*. Garden City, New York: Doubleday, 1959. P. 46.

8. BLEULER, E. *Dementia praecox or the group of schizophrenias*. New York: International Universities Press, 1950.

9. BRAATOY, T. Psychology vs. anatomy in the treatment of "arm neuroses" with physiotherapy. *Journal of Nervous and Mental Disease*, 1952, *115*, 215–245.

10. BRENER, J., & HOTHERSALL, D. Heart rate control under conditions of augmented sensory feedback. *Psychophysiology*, 1966, *3*, 23–28.

11. BRUNSWIK, E. Organismic achievement and environmental probability. *Psychological Review*, 1943, *50*, 255–272.

12. BUCKE, R. M. *Cosmic consciousness.* New Hyde Park, New York: University Books, 1961.

13. BÜHLER, K. *Die Krise der Psychologie.* Jena: G. Fischer, 1927.

14. BYKOV, K. M. *The cerebral cortex and the internal organs.* New York: Chemical, 1957.

15. CAMUS, A. *The fall.* (Transl., J. O'Brien). New York: Vintage, 1956. Pp. 48–49.

16. CARR, G. *Condillac's treatise on the sensations.* Los Angeles: University of Southern California, 1930. P. 3.

17. CARROLL, J. B. (Ed.) *Language, thought and reality. Selected writings of Benjamin Lee Whorf.* New York: Wiley, 1956.

18. CRAIG, W. Male doves reared in isolation. *Journal of Animal Behavior,* 1914, *4,* 121–133.

19. DARWIN, C. *The origin of species.* London: John Murray, 1859.

20. DAVIDOWITZ, J. Personal communication.

21. DELGADO, J. M. R. Emotional behavior in animals and humans. *Psychiatric Research Reports,* 1960, No. 12, 259–266.

22. DOSTOYEVSKY, F. *The brothers Karamazov.* (Transl., C. Garnett). New York: The Modern Library, Random House, 1946. Pp. 251–252.

23. EDDINGTON, A. *The philosophy of physical science.* New York: Macmillan, 1939.

24. ERIKSON, E. H. The problem of ego identity. In M. R. Stein (Ed.), *Identity and anxiety.* Glencoe: Free Press, 1960. Pp. 37–87.

25. FRANK, L. K. Personal communication.

26. FRENKEL-BRUNSWIK, E. Intolerance of ambiguity as an emotional and perceptual personality variable. *Journal of Personality,* 1949–50, *18,* 108–143.

27. FREUD, A. *The ego and the mechanisms of defense.* (Transl., C. Baines). New York: International University Press, 1946.

28. FREUD, S. *The ego and the id.* (Transl., J. Strachey). London: Hogarth Press, 1927.

29. FREUD, S. The interpretation of dreams. In *The basic writings.* New York: Modern Library, 1938.

30. FREUD, S. *Three essays on the theory of sexuality.* (Transl., J. Strachey). New York: Avon Books, 1965.

31. GARDNER, R., HOLZMAN, P. S., KLEIN, G. S., LINTON, H., & SPENCE, D. P. Cognitive control: A study of individual consistencies in behavior. *Psychological Issues,* 1959, *1* (4, Monogr. No. 4), 1–185.

32. GESELL, A., & AMATRUDA, C. *Developmental diagnosis.* (2nd ed.) New York: Hoeber, 1947. P. 29.

33. GIBSON, E. J., & WALK, R. D. The "visual cliff." *The Scientific American,* 1960, *202,* (4), 64–73.

34. GIBSON, J. J. Perception as a function of stimulation. In S. Koch (Ed.), *Psychology: A study of a science.* Vol. 7. New York: McGraw-Hill, 1959.

35. HARLOW, H. F. The development of affectional patterns in infant monkeys. In B. M. Foss (Ed.), *Determinants of infant behavior.* Vol. 1. London: Methuen, 1961.

36. HARTLEY, D. *Observations on man, his frame, his duty, his expectations.* London: 1749.

37. HEBB, D. O. *The organization of behavior.* New York: Wiley, 1949.

38. HEFFERLINE, R. F., KEENAN, B., & HARTFORD, R. Escape and avoidance conditioning in human subjects without observation of their response. *Science,* 1959, *130,* 1338–1339.

39. HELMHOLTZ, H. L. F. *On the sensations of tone.* (4th ed.) New York: Longmans Green, 1912.

40. HELSON, H. *Adaptation-Level theory.* New York: Harper & Row, 1964.

41. HERBART, J. F. *A textbook in psychology.* New York: 1894.

42. HERNÁNDEZ-PEÓN, R., SCHERRER, H., & JOUVET, M. Modification of electrical activity in the cochlear nucleus during "attention" in unanesthesized cats. *Science,* 1956, *123,* 331–332.

43. HERRICK, J. C. *An introduction to neurology.* (5th ed.) Philadelphia: Saunders, 1931.

44. HESS, E. H. Imprinting. *Science,* 1959, *130,* 133–141.

45. HNATIOW, M., & LANG, P. J. Learned stabilization of heart rate. *Psychophysiology,* 1965, *1,* 330–336.

46. HOLT, E. B. The place of illusory experience in a realistic world. In *The new realism.* New York: Macmillan, 1912.

47. HOLZMAN, P. S., & ROUSEY, C. The voice as percept. *Journal of Personality and Social Psychology,* 1966, 4, 79–86.

48. HOLZMAN, P. S., ROUSEY, C., & SNYDER, C. On listening to one's own voice: Effects on psychophysiological responses and free associations. *Journal of Personality and Social Psychology,* 1966, *4,* 432–441.

49. HULL, C. L. *Psychological Monographs,* 1924, *33* (Whole No. 150).

50. HUME, D. An inquiry concerning human understanding. In *Essays and treatises.* (Vol. 3). Basel: J. S. Tourneisen, 1793.

51. JACOBSON, E. Variations of muscular tension (action potential) in man. *American Journal of Physiology,* 1940, *129,* 388 (Abstract).

52. JAMES, W. *The principles of psychology.* Vol. 1. New York: Holt, 1890.

53. JAMES, W. *The principles of psychology.* Vol. 2. New York: Holt, 1890.

54. JAMES, W. *Varieties of religious experience.* New York: The Modern Library, Random House, 1929.

55. JANET, P. On memories which are too real. In C. M. Campbell, et al. (Eds.), *Problems of personality.* New York: Harcourt, Brace, 1925. Pp. 139–150.

56. JUNG, C. G. *Psychological types.* (Transl., H. G. Baynes). New York: Harcourt, Brace, 1923.

57. KAMIYA, J. Conditioned introspection: Humans can learn to detect and control their EEG alpha rhythms. Paper read

at the annual meeting of the Society for Psychophysiological Research, Washington, D.C., October, 1964.

58. KANT, I. *The critique of pure reason.* Riga: Hartknoch, 1781.

59. KILPATRICK, F. P. Two processes in perceptual learning. *Journal of Experimental Psychology,* 1954, *47* (No. 5), 1954, 362–370.

60. KLEIN, G. S. Need and regulation. In M. R. Jones (Ed.), *Nebraska Symposium on Motivation.* Lincoln: University of Nebraska Press, 1956. Pp. 224–274.

61. KLEITMAN, N. *Sleep and wakefulness.* Chicago: University of Chicago Press, 1963.

62. KOFFKA, K. *Principles of gestalt psychology.* New York: Harcourt, Brace, 1935.

63. KOHLER, I. The formation and transformation of the perceptual world. *Psychological Issues,* 1963, *3* (4, Monogr. No. 12), 1–173.

64. KRECH, D., ROSENZWEIG, M. R., & BENNETT, E. L. Effects of environmental complexity and training on brain chemistry. *Journal of Comparative Physiological Psychology,* 1960, *53,* 509–519.

65. LASKI, MARGHANITA. *Ecstasy: A study of some secular and religious experiences.* Bloomington: Indiana University Press, 1961.

66. LECKY, P. *Self-consistency: a theory of personality.* New York: Island Press, 1945.

67. LERNER, E. New techniques for tracing cultural factors in children's personality organization. Paper presented at meeting of the Society for Research in Child Development, December, 1936.

68. LISINA, M. I. The role orientation in the transformation of involuntary reactions into voluntary ones. In L. G. Voronin, et al. (Eds.), *Orienting reflex and exploratory behavior.* Baltimore: American Institute of Biological Sciences, 1965, 450–456.

69. LORENZ, K. The nature of instinct. In C. H. Schiller (Ed.), *Instinctive behavior*. New York: International Press, 1957.

70. LUND, F. H. The psychology of belief. *Journal of Abnormal and Social Psychology*, 1925, *20*, 63–81.

71. McNAMARA, H. J. Non-veridical perception as a function of rewards and punishments. *Perceptual and Motor Skills*, 1959, *9*, 67–80. (Monogr. Suppl. No. 2).

72. McNAMARA, H. J., & FISCH, R. I. Personal space and laterality in perception. *Perceptual and Motor Skills*, 1960, *10*, 70–73.

73. MALMO, R. B. Classical and instrumental conditioning with septal stimulation as reinforcement. *Journal of Comparative and Physiological Psychology*, 1965, *60*, (1), 1–8.

74. MANNHEIM, K. *Ideology and utopia: An introduction to the sociology of knowledge*. New York: Harcourt, Brace, 1936.

75. MAKAROV, P. O. A study of interoception in human subjects. *Uchen. Zap. Leningr. U., Ser. Biol.*, 1950, *22* (123), 345–368.

76. MASEFIELD, J. *Selected poems*. New York: Macmillan, 1923. Pp. 136–137.

77. MAX, L. W. Experimental study of the motor theory of consciousness. *Psychological Bulletin*, 1933, *30*, 714–731.

78. MEYER, E., & COVI, L. The experience of depersonalization: A written report by a patient. *Psychiatry*, 1960, *23*, 215–217.

79. MOORE, H. T. The genetic aspects of consonance and dissonance. *Psychological Monographs*, 1914, *17* (Whole No. 73).

80. MURPHY, G., & KLEMME, H. L. Unfinished business. *Journal of the American Society for Psychical Research*, 1966, *60* (4), pp. 306–307.

81. MURRAY, H. A. Personal communication.

82. OLDS, J., & MILNER, P. Positive reinforcement produced by electrical stimulation of septal area and other regions of

the rat brain. *Journal of Comparative and Physiological Psychology*, 1954, 47, 419–427.

83. ORWELL, G. *1984.* New York: New World Library, 1960.

84. OSGOOD, C. E. Studies on the generality of affective meaning systems. *American Psychologist*, 1960, *17*, 10–28.

85. PAVLOV, I. P. *Lectures on conditioned reflexes.* New York: International Publishers, 1928.

86. PENFIELD, W. Memory mechanisms. *Archives of Neurology and Psychiatry*, 1952, *67*, p. 183.

87. PENFIELD, W. *Epilepsy and the functional anatomy of the human brain.* Boston: Little, Brown, 1954.

88. PFAFFMAN, C. De Gustibus. *The American Psychologist*, 1965, *20*, 21–33.

89. PIAGET, J. *The construction of reality in the child.* New York: Basic Books, 1954.

90. PIAGET, J. *Les mécanismes perceptifs.* Paris: Presses Universitaires de France, 1961.

91. POLYAK, S., & WILLNER, E. N. Retinal structure and color vision. *Docum. Opthal., Garvenh.*, 1949, *3*, 24–56.

92. RAPAPORT, D. Toward a theory of thinking. In D. Rapaport (Ed.), *Organization and pathology of thought.* New York: Columbia University Press, 1951. Pp. 689–730.

93. RAZRAN, G. Extinction re-examined and re-analyzed: A new theory. *Psychological Review*, 1956, *63* (1), 39–52.

94. RAZRAN, G. The observable unconscious and the inferrable conscious in current Soviet psychophysiology: Interoceptive conditioning, semantic conditioning and the orienting reflex. *Psychological Review*, 1961, *68* (2), 81–147.

95. REICH, W. *Character-Analysis.* New York: Orgone Institute Press, 1949.

96. ROSENZWEIG, S. The effect of male hormone medication on sex responses on the Thematic Apperception Test. Paper presented at the meetings of the Eastern Psychological Association, New York, April, 1942.

97. RUSSELL, B. *Mysticism and logic.* New York: W. W. Norton, 1929. Pp. 47–48.

98. SANTOS, J. F., FARROW, B. J., HAINES, J. R., & MCNAMARA, H. J. Studies of perceptual learning and perceptual selectivity. Unpublished manuscript, 1967.

99. SCOTT, J. P. Critical periods in behavior development. *Science,* 1962, *138,* 949–957.

100. SEVERN, J. Letter. E. Gurney, F. W. H. Myers, & F. Podmore. *Phantasms of the living.* Vol. 1. London: Trubner, 1886. P. 188.

101. SHERRINGTON, C. *The integrative action of the nervous system.* New Haven: Yale University Press, 1948.

102. SIMPSON, G. G. *The meaning of evolution.* New Haven: Yale University Press, 1949.

103. SMITH, K. U., SHERMAN, A., & SMITH, W. M. Sensory feedback analysis in medical research. I. Delayed sensory feedback in behavior and neural functions. *American Journal of Physical Medicine,* 1963, *42* (No. 6), 228–262.

104. SMOCK, C. D., & HOLT, B. G. Children's reactions to novelty: An experimental study of "curiosity motivation." *Child Development,* 1962, *33,* 631–642.

105. SNYDER, F. W., & PRONKO, N. H. *Vision with spatial inversion.* Wichita: Wichita University Press, 1952.

106. SOKOLOV, N. YE. *Perception and the conditioned reflex.* New York: Macmillan, 1963.

107. SPENCE, D. P., & HOLLAND, B. The restricting effects of awareness: A paradox and explanation. *Journal of Abnormal and Social Psychology,* 1963, *64* (3), 163–174.

108. SPENCE, K. W. Theoretical interpretations of learning. In S. Stevens (Ed.), *Handbook of experimental psychology.* New York: Wiley, 1951.

109. SPITZ, R. A. *The first year of life.* New York: International Universities Press, 1965.

110. STERN, W. *Allgemeine psychologie.* Haag: Martinus Nijhoff, 1935.

111. TANNEGAY DE QUÉNETAIN. Origines et aboutissements du pouvoir de la musique. *Realités,* No. 141, 1957, 86–117.

112. TAYLOR, B. Personal document. In J. M. Peebles (Ed.) *Seers of the ages.* New York: 1869. Pp. 225–226.

113. THORNDIKE, E. L. *The fundamentals of learning.* New York: Teachers College, Columbia University, 1932.

114. TITCHENER, E. *Lectures on the elementary psychology of feeling and attention.* New York: Macmillan, 1908.

115. UEXKÜLL, J. J. *Theoretical biology.* (Transl., D. L. Mackinnon). Harcourt, Brace, 1926.

116. USEEM, J. Personal communication.

117. VOTH, H., & MAYMAN, M. A dimension of personality organization. *Archives of General Psychiatry,* 1963, *8,* 366–380.

118. WENGER, M. A., BAGCHI, B. K., & ANAND, B. K. Experiments in India on "voluntary" control of heart rate and pulse. *Circulation,* 1961, *24,* 1319–1325.

119. WHITEHEAD, A. N. *Process and reality.* New York: Harper, 1960.

120. WIENER, N. *Cybernetics.* New York: Wiley, 1949.

121. WIESEL, T. N., & HUBEL, D. H. Effects of visual deprivation on morphology and physiology in the cat's lateral geniculate body. *Journal of Neurophysiology,* 1963, *26,* 978–992.

122. WOODWORTH, R. S. Reinforcement of perception. *American Journal of Psychology,* 1947, *60,* 119–124.

123. YENSEN, R. Some factors affecting taste sensitivity in man. *The Quarterly Journal of Experimental Psychology,* 1959, *11,* 230–238.

124. ZENER, K. The significance of behavior accompanying conditioned salivary secretion for theories of the conditioned response. *American Journal of Psychology,* 1937, *50,* 384–403.

Name Index

Subject Index